A Brief History

Of The Baptists

BY EDWARD H. OVERBEY

D1572158

THE CHALLENGE PRESS
P. O. BOX 5567
LITTLE ROCK, ARKANSAS 72205

P. O. Box 5567
Little Rock, Arkansas 72215

Table Of Contents

Dedication

This book is
dedicated
to my faithful Baptist parents,
Pastor and Mrs. Hafford H. Overbey

Foreword

I consider it a privilege to write a few words of introduction to this splendid short history of the Baptists. There are several very commendable features possessed by this book. First, it is very readable. I found myself reading right on through the manuscript with keen enjoyment. Second, it gives the essential facts concerning our Baptist people in such condensed form as to enable the average reader to know the things that he would probably never learn if he had to peruse lengthy volumes of Baptist history. The average Baptist church member of this day knows little about the thrilling and heroic history of his people, or else he would hold them in greater appreciation. The reading of this book should be like a "shot in the arm" to all such. Likewise those not Baptists will gain a greater appreciation concerning the people called Baptists through reading this book. In the third place, the book deals fairly with the facts of Baptist history. The objective attitude of the unbiased historian is maintained.

This book should be in Baptist homes and certainly it should be in the library of every Baptist church. It contains information that every Baptist should have, and in such brief readable form as to be ideal for common use. The person who gets a good grasp of the facts presented in this volume, will have to discard the careless attitude that gives rise to the saying, "It doesn't matter which church one belongs to." Our Baptist ancestors endured dungeon, fire and sword to hold true to the truths that have been passed down to us. A reading of this book will inspire added loyalty to those truths that cost our heroic ancestors so very much.

I predict for this book a good circulation. Many will come to feel greatly indebted to Mr. Overbey for his splendid work.

Sincerely,
Roy Mason

Preface

As the author of this book I would like to acknowledge the valuable help that I have received. Several have read the manuscript and have given helpful suggestions that were followed in most cases. Pastor Louis Maple has been particularly helpful in this regard and in bringing this book to be printed.

For some time we have felt the need for a short history of the Baptists that deals more with our history of the past 300 years than most do of this size. We pray that this book might be helpful to all and might bring glory to God.

Introduction

SELECTING THE MATERIAL

In writing a history of a group of people as large and as old as the Baptists we have a problem in selecting the material to use. What should we omit and what should we use? There is a great quantity of good material but it cannot all be used if the work is to have an end. There are many faithful churches and individuals that have played an important part in our history but they can not all be recognized. We have sought to mention the churches, individuals, associations, events, etc. which have had an influence on the Baptists as a whole or a large segment of the Baptists. Some churches, individuals, etc. have been mentioned as examples of what we found in Baptist history. In doing this many churches and persons have not been mentioned who may be more important and greater in the eyes of the Lord. Even though we cannot mention them all by name, we recognize all of them as having a part in this great history in which we can only briefly outline the highlights.

DETERMINING THE SUBJECT

Our subject is the Baptists. By this we do not mean a particular association or convention. There are several large conventions and associations. There are also some churches that are not in any organization with other churches. Our subject is larger than any particular group of Baptist churches and much older since all of the associations and conventions of today are relatively young.

By this we do not mean only the people called by this name. This is not a history of the Baptist name. Some churches that we will write about were called by other names before they were called Baptists. The day they were called Baptists saw no change among them other than a new designation. Some people have changed their name. One day a man is called Smith but the next day he legally changes his name and he is called Brown. He is the same person; the only difference is his name. To write Brown's biography you would have to go further back than the day his name was changed. To write a history of the Baptists you must go further back than the first time they were called Baptists.

By this we do mean a people that hold to certain belief and practices who are now called Baptists. We seek to write a history of this people. Their names and organizations are only a part of their history.

STATING THE DOCTRINE

Baptist Confessions — What are these beliefs and practices of the Baptists? There are two well-known Baptist confessions of faith, The Philadelphia and The New Hampshire. The Philadelphia Confession is much larger and more explicit than the New Hampshire. The New Hampshire is in harmony with the Philadelphia but not as detailed. These confessions state well the beliefs of the Baptists. Even though many churches have never formally accepted one of these confessions their basic beliefs and practices when examined are in harmony with them. Even though some today have deviated from these doctrines and still retain the name, Baptist, we believe, they are a small minority and are generally recognized as unorthodox by the Baptists as a whole.

Two Classes of Doctrine — Baptist doctrine might be divided into two classes for the sake of convenience. The doctrines that we hold in common with most of the other major denominations such as the doctrines of God, Christ, Sin, etc. would be in one class. The other class would be the doctrines that we hold as our distinctives.

Baptist Distinctives — Some of these Baptist distinctives are held by other denominations but only Baptists hold them all in the way we interpret them. Our distinctives might be stated briefly as follows:

1. The Bible is the final authority for faith and practice.
2. Salvation is by grace through faith in Christ alone.

3. Baptism is the voluntary immersion of a believer in Christ to symbolically show what Christ has done for him.
4. The Lord's Supper is symbolic only.
5. A church should be composed of only professed believers who have been Scripturally baptized.
6. Each church is self-governing and democratic under the command of its Head, Jesus Christ.

Implied Doctrines — These distinctives have been stated differently by Baptists from time to time but the basic ideas remain the same. The difference is only in statement. For example, religious freedom is a belief of the Baptists but we have not stated it separately since it is involved in the distinctives stated. If a church governs itself and a person must make the decision to profess his faith in Christ and ask for baptism, then religious freedom is automatically involved. The separation of church and state is also involved.

Under these distinctives there can be no church officer that can govern several self-governing churches. This is an impossibility. This rules out such unscriptural offices as Pope and Archbishop and helps to define the true meaning of Bishop, Elder, and Deacon as used in the New Testament. Neither can there be an officer that can interfere with the responsibility of each member in a democratic church. It is also implied that a church is a local, visible body and that there may Scripturally be many churches around the world as long as they are the same kind in belief and practice.

The Final Authority — Many denominations believe in the complete inspiration of the Bible but few actually believe and practice the Bible as the final authority for faith and practice. This is a distinctive of the Baptists. This does not mean that we cannot have a Sunday School because it is not explicitly stated in the Bible. We can have a Sunday School because the principle of teaching the Bible to all ages is commanded in the Scriptures. We might carry that principle out in several ways as long as in doing so we do not violate any principles of the Bible. Those who claim the Bible as a final authority and baptize unbelieving infants violate their professed final authority. The Bible never gives one example of baptizing unbelieving infants. It denies such a practice when it commands us to baptize believers and gives only examples of baptizing professed believers.

Salvation by Grace — A number of different churches profess to believe that salvation is by grace through faith in Christ, but when carefully examined something else is often added as necessary. Grace and faith are defined differently in some cases than the Bible defines them. Baptists believe that salvation is a gift of God to undeserving sinners. There is not one thing in the sinner to merit it. The sinner receives salvation by faith alone and there is no merit in the faith. The salvation that God gives and the sinner receives by faith is Christ who was perfect in every way and died to suffer the penalty due our sins. When we receive this salvation we are saved for all eternity and we cannot be lost for we are kept by God's grace. Nothing the sinner ever does in any way merits or helps him to keep this salvation. The sinner who is saved will seek to serve God out of love for Him. There will be spiritual fruit in his life but this has nothing to do with saving him or keeping him saved. This statement is only a summary of what Baptists have stated in the Philadelphia and New Hampshire Confessions but it is still explicit enough to show what we mean when we mention the distinctive that salvation is by grace through faith in Christ.

Baptism — Concerning the distinctive of baptism we contend that the word means immerse or dip and that this is the only Scriptural mode. Some others will accept immersion and even practice it but they believe there are other modes such as sprinkling or pouring also. We contend it is only for professed believers. We say that infants cannot understand the gospel, cannot believe the gospel, and cannot profess to believe the gospel. Labored theological explanations as to how they can do these things are not convincing to Baptists. The Bible is clear as to what it means by professed believers and we accept no other explanation. We believe that baptism is only a picture of our death and resurrection in Christ. It has no saving value.

The Lord's Supper — Concerning the Lord's supper, most denominations are agreed as to the elements and most believe it is only to be taken after baptism. The controversy is actually over baptism which we have already discussed. If others agreed concerning baptism we would also basically agree concerning who is eligible to participate in the supper. Our distinctive belief on this point is that the supper is only symbolical. It is to remind us of what Jesus did for us until He comes. It is to remind us that Jesus Christ is the constant source of our spiritual life. Several other denominations believe it is more than symbolism. They believe in varying degrees that grace comes actually in participating in the supper. Some believe that the bread and wine are actually changed into the literal body and blood of Christ.

Requirements for Church Membership — Another distinctive is the membership requirement. Only professed believers whò have been Scripturally baptized have met the membership requirement. What is meant by believers and Scriptural baptism has been explained under the distinctives concerning salvation and baptism. If those who differ with Baptists were agreed on those points the membership requirement of a church would not be a distinctive.

Church Government — There are a number of different types of governments found among the various denominations. Baptists have contended that each church is self-governing, meaning that each is independent of other sister churches and also the civil government. This does not mean that churches agreed in doctrine cannot have fellowship or join together in Scriptural causes in a way that does not violate the principle of self-government. Neither does it mean that the civil government cannot regulate them with regard to building codes, property laws, and other matters pertaining to civil government. However, the government must not interfere with the work of the great commission. The church conducts its business in a democratic way; each member has a governmental responsibility.

Conclusion — Although there may be a few other churches holding to several of these distinctives along with the Baptists, only the Baptists hold to all of these distinctives. The holding of these distinctives along with the doctrines that we hold in common with the major denominations makes a church a Baptist church. This does not mean that all Baptist churches are identical. There are differences on some matters but not on these basic principles that have been stated. We have given the beliefs of the people we will write about but we have not given the Scriptural proofs.

GIVING THE PROOF

Scripture for the final authority — Since the doctrines we hold in common with most major denominations are considered by them to be taught in the Bible we will seek to prove only that the Baptist distinctives are taught in the Bible. The Bible is full of statements to the effect that it is the final authority for faith and practice. Individuals and churches are supposed to follow it. Note these Scriptures: Isa. 8:20; 2 Tim. 3:15-17; Eph. 5:23-24; Eph. 2:20; James 1:21-22. Isaiah makes it clear that God's Word is the final authority and standard. If a person's words are not in harmony with it, that one is considered as having no light in him. This is a most serious judgment. Although the New Testament was not written at this time, nor part of the Old Testament, yet the principle remains just as true. This truth applies to all of God's Word, even the books which had not been written at that time. The passage in 2 Tim. has a context which is most instructive. Timothy is warned of those who will deviate from the truth in belief and practice and he is commended to Paul's doctrine which was spoken and which was written in His epistles and to the Old Testament as being the means "that the man of God may be perfect, throughly furnished unto all good works." This passage makes it clear that a Christian's final authority and standard is the Bible. What is true of an individual Christian here certainly applies to a group of Christians organized into a church.

Jesus is the head of each man and each New Testament church and consequently each man and each church should be subject to Him. What the Head says should be final. The Bible is His word and therefore the final authority. Ephesians 2:20 should be carefully studied. The apostles and prophets were the ones called to put God's Word into writing. The first century was a time when the final teachings of God through His Son were made known and God had them written in the New Testament. The special offices of apostle and prophet were given this task and when the work was done the offices were no longer needed. We only proclaim the finished message today.

We do not add to it. Some passages represent the church as built on Christ. He is the final authority and therefore the basis or foundation of each of His churches. The apostles and prophets in writing the New Testament wrote of Him; He is the subject of the New Testament. The foundation or authority of each church then can be said to be the apostles and prophets. Just as the Old Testament is referred to as "Moses and the Prophets" at times, so the New Testament is spoken of as "the apostles and the prophets." The passage in James and many others refer to the written Word of God as our guide.

Scripture for Salvation by Grace — Salvation in the Scriptures is a very clearly revealed doctrine. Romans 3:10 states that all are unrighteous and this passage goes on to describe every sinner as being depraved completely and unable to save himself and unworthy in himself to receive salvation. Such Scripture verses as Romans 3:19-23; 5:6-8; Romans 3:24-26; 2 Cor. 5:21; 1 Peter 2:24, and 3:18 make it very clear that salvation is in Christ because He took our sins and suffered for them, paying our sin debt in full. He did it all; we did nothing. Romans 4:1-8 and Eph. 2:8-10 state that salvation is not received by works, but by faith and if there were any works involved on our part it could not be grace, for that would be a contradiction. Works and debt go together, not works and grace. Grace and faith go together for there is no merit in faith. Even faith is a gift of God. A careful study of these passages makes it clear what is meant by grace and faith. There is no excuse for confusing the two with any type of merit or works on man's part. Ephesians states that we work after we are saved. Jesus said to saved people, "If ye love me keep my commandments." John 14:1, 2, 3, 15. The Bible represents obedience to Christ's commands as fruits in one's life and good works as coming properly from a motive of love to Christ. Works are never represented for the purpose of obtaining salvation. Salvation in the Bible is represented as eternal and something that cannot be lost once a person has it. John 10:27-30; 1 Peter 1:3-5.

Meaning of Baptism — Among scholars there seems to be an almost unanimous opinion that the word baptize and kindred words in the New Testament mean immerse or dip. The word baptize is a transliteration of the Greek word

Baptizo. King James of England in giving instructions to the translators of our King James Bible specifically stated that the word was not to be translated and this has been followed ever since. Although people may use the word today to mean sprinkle, pour, etc. this will not change what it meant when the New Testament was written and that is what we are interested in. Our meaning should be what we find in the New Testament days.

In Webster's Collegiate Dictionary, fifth edition, put out by the G. and C. Merriam Co. of Springfield, Massachusetts, it states that the word baptize comes from a Greek word meaning "to dip in water." All the standard Greek lexicons, such as Liddell and Scott's Lexicon and Thayer's Lexicon, state that the word in the New Testament means to dip or immerse. Scholars of other denominations than Baptist admit this is the New Testament meaning. Even John Wesley, Martin Luther, and John Calvin admitted that this is the meaning in the New Testament.

The contexts of the New Testament demand the meaning immerse. John 3:23 speaks of "much water" in connection with the ordinance. Acts 8:38, 39 tells us that both the candidate and the administrator went into water to perform the ordinance and then came out of the water. The symbolism also demands this meaning when it says in Romans 6:4, 5 that we are "buried with him by baptism" and "if we have been planted together in the likeness of his death, we shall be also in the likeness of his resurrection."

Subjects of Baptism — Many passages teach that only professed believers were baptized. Three examples would be John 4:1, Acts 8:12, and Acts 18:8. Those that believe unbelieving infants should be baptized can only point to several passages that speak of whole families being baptized and assume there must have been infants in those families. The New Testament does not give one case of an infant being baptized. We believe these families were composed of people old enough to understand the gospel and that they professed faith in Christ and then were baptized. This harmonizes with the rest of the teachings of the New Testament. To teach otherwise is to make the Scripture contradict itself. The contexts of some of these passages make it clear that the whole family was old enough to believe and did so. Acts 16:34 indicates that all of the

Philippian jailer's house believed.

Purpose of Baptism — The Bible teaches that baptism is a "likeness" in Romans 6:4-5. 1 Peter 3:21 mentions baptism as a "like figure." Baptism is a picture of what Christ did for us. He died, was buried, and rose again. Since He was our substitute this was our death, burial, and resurrection. In baptism we give a picture of how we were saved. The Bible gives examples of individuals that were saved but not baptized, showing that baptism is not necessary to salvation but is only symbolic. Luke 23:39-43 tells of the salvation of the thief on the cross without baptism. Abraham is represented in Luke 16 as in Heaven and he was never baptized. Acts 16:30-31 answers the question how to be saved by saying, "Believe on the Lord Jesus Christ." Baptism is not mentioned in answering this question.

Misunderstood Scriptures on Baptism — Even though the Scriptures are so plain on the subject yet some introduce passages of the Bible and interpret them in such a way as to contradict these plain statements. There are some Scriptures that appear to some to teach that baptism is necessary to salvation. But when these are carefully examined and studied in connection with other passages it is seen that they do not teach such a thing. Acts 22:16 is an example of these Scriptures. It says, "arise and be baptized and wash away thy sins." This does not mean literally but only symbolically. The real death, burial, and resurrection of Christ is what literally washes away our sins. Baptism pictures the death, burial, and resurrection of Christ and so washes away one's sins symbolically. To teach otherwise would be to contradict many other passages in the Bible. The Bible uses such language many times and we understand it without any trouble. If the contexts of these passages that are used to teach that baptism is necessary for salvation are examined, most of the passages will clear themselves up without any further study.

Scripture for the Lord's Supper — The Lord's Supper is represented in the New Testament as a symbolic ordinance having no saving value. Some contend with the Baptists on this point stating that it is more than symbolic. When Jesus said, "this is my body" and "this is my blood" we believe that He was speaking figuratively not literally,

18

Matt. 26:26-28. Jesus said that He was this or that many times and all of us realize that He was speaking figuratively, John 8:12; 10:7, 11. 1 Cor. 11:24-26 makes it plain that it is "in remembrance" of the Lord. It also says, "As often as ye eat this bread and drink this cup, ye do shew the Lord's death till he come." It says, "shew" or we might say, "picture." The supper is obviously symbolic only.

Scripture for Church Membership Requirements — The churches of the New Testament were composed only of professed believers who had been Scripturally baptized. Peter preached the message of salvation on the day of Pentecost and Acts 2:41 says, "Then they that gladly received his word were baptized: and the same day there were added unto them about three thousand souls." Three thousand listening to Peter's message gladly received his message or were saved and then they were baptized and added to the church at Jerusalem. The context in Acts we believe will easily bear out this interpretation.

The epistles written to churches speak of the people in the churches as saved people. The terms given to them belong only to the professed believer. The epistles in speaking of baptism imply that it was something that all in the churches had experienced. The commission in Matt. 28:18-20 implies that all converts are to be baptized. The practice of the New Testament preachers was to win converts and then baptize them. All who professed seemed to be baptized without exception unless they died before it was possible. This is why Baptists insist on this distinctive.

Scripture for Church Government — Each church was self-governing and democratic. Paul rebuked the Corinthian Church, 1 Cor. 5, and urged them to discipline one of their members for immorality but the passage implies the action would have to be the church's and no one else's. Paul does not appeal to Peter or the apostles or the church at Jerusalem or some council, for such had no jurisdiction over the Corinthian Church. The epistles show each church governed itself according to the teachings of the Lord. Acts 6:2-5 is an example to show that each church governed itself democratically.

FINDING THE BEGINNING
Since the beliefs and practices of the Baptists are

found in the New Testament the obvious conclusion is that the churches of the New Testament were Baptist churches and that Baptist history must begin in the first century. After examining the churches in the New Testament what would we call them if they were lifted out of the New Testament times and placed in some of our American cities today? We believe that the only thing we could call them would be Baptist Churches.

ANSWERING THE OBJECTIONS

There are certain objections that might be made when Baptists claim that the churches of the New Testament were Baptist in doctrine and practice. We would like to consider those objections.

First Objection — It might be stated that Baptists are not perfect so how can their churches be considered New Testament and how can New Testament churches be called Baptist? It is readily admitted that Baptists are not perfect, not one of them. In fact no person is perfect in this life because he still sins even after being a Christian for many years. Of course no church made up of Christians could be perfect either. But this is also true of the Christians in the Scriptures. Even though the Christians in the New Testament were not perfect they did believe and seek to practice certain doctrines. These churches were considered by the Lord to be His churches. If imperfect people then could believe and practice certain doctrines and be considered to be the Lord's churches, then we believe that imperfect people now can do the same and be considered to be the Lord's churches.

Second Objection — Another objection comes out of the type of reasoning that follows. If churches in the New Testament were not perfect and were still considered to be the Lord's, perhaps a church can be far off in doctrine today and still be a New Testament church. Perhaps many of the churches of other denominations are considered New Testament by the Lord. If this is so why don't the Baptists consider others to be the Lord's churches also? We answer that it is true that the Lord does not tell us how far from the faith and practice of the New Testament we can be and still be considered a church of His. He does tell us though in the New Testament what one of His churches should be.

We should seek to follow this pattern perfectly. We should strive for the maximum and what we know is right and not for a minimum and what is wrong or doubtful. Our distinctives we believe are clearly taught in the Bible so we must follow them and work with and approve only churches that follow them. Other teachings contrary to these, and those who hold them, must be condemned if we are to be true to the Lord. If some of these are still considered His churches, He is the only one that knows it, for He has not left us anything in His Word to inform us on the subject. We must act on what He has said, not on His silence.

Third Objection — Some would object to our being New Testament churches because we have omitted certain doctrines and practices. Since we do not speak in tongues or perform miracles of healing we are not New Testament churches, they say. We do not believe these gifts were to continue but were only for the first century when they were used for the purpose of accrediting the first churches and those who wrote the New Testament. The New Testament has been accredited and accepted and the first churches have been accredited and accepted as from God. The purpose was accomplished so the special gifts are no longer needed. The Bible teaches that certain gifts were to continue while others were to cease. 1 Cor. 13:8, Heb. 2:3-4, Acts 2, 1 Cor. 14:1-33.

We also would add that none have these gifts today and none have had them since the New Testament days. Some think they have but they are mistaken. When their so-called speaking in tongues and miracles are compared with the Scriptures we find they are not the same. Do the ones that claim these gifts speak in a foreign tongue suddenly, having never studied the language before? Are they understood by people using the tongue? Or do they make unidentifiable sounds which are not like any language in the world today? Do they heal lepers where the flesh is rotting and they are made whole? Do they raise the dead? Or do they heal of diseases that cannot be actually proven by doctors that they exist? Or do they heal of ills that were brought on by emotional disturbances that others could duplicate knowing certain facts about the human mind? Some say that the person to be healed must have faith but what faith did the dead have that were raised in the Bible? The gifts claimed by some today are quite different from those experienced by New Testament Christians. Yes, God can and does heal today but He has not promised to heal as He did in the New Testament. God heals today by means of doctors and medicine and sometimes apart from any means in answer to the prayers of His people. Baptists believe in "Divine healing" but not the kind that is usually associated with those words.

Fourth Objection — It is also objected that when Baptists believe they are New Testament churches they often have a poor attitude towards people of other denominations. Sometimes some Baptists do have a poor attitude and this is wrong. Those who are guilty should change in their poor attitude but not in any truth that they hold. However our attitude might not always be understood. We believe error must be condemned and we have many Scriptures that teach us so. Doctrines contrary to our distinctives must be condemned like any other error.

Our attitude does not mean that only Baptists are saved. We believe that anyone who believes on Jesus Christ as his personal Savior is saved and is a child of God no matter to which church he might belong. He need not be a member of any church to be saved.

Our attitude does not mean that we have no love for other Christians or cannot have fellowship with them. We can have Christian fellowship with other Christians but we cannot have church fellowship since we cannot agree as to the way God wants us to serve Him and to worship Him. One member of a family may condemn another when one believes the other wrong and still love him. This is true of Baptists when they protest against the doctrinal errors of others and still love them.

Our attitude does not mean that no one else has ever accomplished anything for the Lord but Baptists. We believe that God used John Calvin, Martin Luther, George Whitefield, and many others. We believe that God will bless His truth whenever it is used. These men had some truth and God blessed it but they had some error on the doctrine of the church. We do not believe God approved of that. We are to follow all of the truth of the Bible even if some great men did not.

Our attitude does not mean that no other church can

be a New Testament church. We believe all who will pattern their church after the New Testament will be New Testament churches and we urge others to do this. Nothing stops them but themselves. These errors in church doctrine can be corrected.

Fifth Objection — It is also objected that the Baptists cannot truly judge whether they began in the New Testament since the judgment involves themselves. It is true that the Scriptures teach us that on some things such as motives we cannot fully judge ourselves or others. But it also teaches us that on other things we can and should judge ourselves. We should check ourselves to see that we are following the plain teachings of Scriptures. The distinctives that we mentioned are such that a person can judge to see if the Scriptures teach them and if he is following them. The Bible is clear that this kind of judging is possible.

Support for Baptist Distinctives by Non-Baptists — It is true also that these distinctives have been recognized as taught in the New Testament by many scholars of all the major denominations. We have not the space in this work but we could quote historians, commentators, linguists, etc. of the Roman Catholics, Episcopalians, Lutherans, Presbyterians, Methodists, etc. that would admit our claims. Not one perhaps would admit all of the distinctives but all of the distinctives would be admitted by them together. There are various reasons why these scholars do not follow these teachings themselves. Some believe these can be changed because their church has the authority, or the climate permits it, or the age demands it, or for some other reason.

OUTLINING THE HISTORY

We have divided our history into four periods and designated each by a term that describes some major characteristic of that period. They are as follows:

The Period of Establishment	27 — 100
The Period of Apostasy	100 — 313
The Period of Obscurity	313 — 1638
The Period of Toleration	1638 — 1960

Periods Summarized — The dates are not meant to be infallible. They represent events that happened as near as we can tell in those years. The Period of Establishment is the period from the time the Lord founded the first church to the death of the last apostle, John, who wrote the last book of the New Testament. This was a period for organizing and developing the first churches which would be the patterns for future churches.

The Period of Apostasy ended with Constantine favoring and influencing the churches. It was a time when the errors of Catholicism were developing as New Testament churches deviated from the New Testament pattern. All the basic parts of the Catholic system were finished by the end of this period. It needed only the Roman Church as its head to complete the basic system. It was a time when the faithful New Testament churches were going into obscurity.

The Period of Obscurity began with Constantine's acceptance of Christianity and his linking of the government with the apostate churches. It was a time of great persecution for New Testament churches. Records were destroyed and it is difficult to tell the Baptist story other than as a martyrology. Professed Christians persecuted New Testament churches. Much of the story was told by the enemies of the Baptists who did not understand their beliefs and practices.

The Period of Toleration began with the rise of the English and American churches that left records which enable us to write a complete and continuous history of the Baptists from that day until now. During this period toleration was a blessing that most Baptists enjoyed. It was not always the best toleration but it was present most of the time, distinguishing this period from all others.

The Period Of Establishment: 27-100

THE FOUNDING OF THE CHURCH

My Church — The first time the word "church" appears in the New Testament is in Matt. 16:18 and Jesus uses it. The word "church" has a host of meanings today but in the New Testament the Greek word it represents, ekklesia, means assembly or congregation. Jesus said, "I will build my church." There were other assemblies in existence at the time which had their own beliefs and purposes such as the assemblies in the Greek cities that carried on their governmental affairs. For this reason Jesus says, "my church" to distinguish it from other kinds. He was to give it beliefs and a mission that would make it unique and peculiarly His own.

Meaning of Word "Church" in Matt. 16:18 — The language in this passage is such that a person reading it cannot help but realize that the church spoken of is a great institution. These grand statements have influenced some to think that Jesus uses the word "church" in a new sense. Something much more than assembly is meant and something much more than the churches at Corinth, Ephesus, and Antioch are referred to, they think. Much depends on how you look at these churches. If you look at the individual members and all their imperfections and nothing more, you will be very disappointed with each one. But if you look at them as composed of saved sinners that Jesus suffered for, as sinners whose lives have been completely changed since receiving Christ, as people preaching Christ to the world and administering Divinely given ordinances, you will see that these churches are greater and more important than any institution on earth.

To change the meaning of a word you must have good evidence that the speaker or writer of that word intended it that way. A basic principle that all scholars recognize is that a word must retain its usual meaning as long as the word used makes good sense that way. Only when it will not make good sense are we allowed to give it a new or rare meaning. If we apply this principle in this passage we will see that "assembly" makes good sense so we cannot agree with those who would try to change the meaning here. Some might argue that Jesus says "church" which is singular and not churches, plural. We answer that Jesus uses the word in a generic sense speaking of His church as a class of which there were to be many representatives in the future. When God said, "Let us make man," He used "man" in the singular for He was speaking of a kind of creature that was distinct from other kinds of creatures. By the singular He did not intend for us to believe there would be only one particular man in the world. There have been many men but all are of one kind which is distinct from the other kinds of God's creatures.

Jesus used the word "church" twenty-three times, twenty times in Revelation and three times in Matthew. Twenty-two times there is agreement among all that the word means assembly. It is either plural or the context is very clear so that there can be no doubt in any mind that it is speaking of a local, visible body. Matthew 16:18 is the only place where some think it has a new meaning. But if Jesus used the word twenty-two times and there is no question concerning its meaning then it seems that we must believe that the one remaining place has the same meaning. In this one place the ordinary meaning makes good sense and the context does not indicate a new sense. If Jesus used the word here in a new sense, as some say, then you would have the Lord saying He would build a church and then never mentioning it again but instead mentioning another church twenty-two times that He never said anything about building. This would not be like the Lord.

The Rock Foundation of the Church — This passage goes on to say that Jesus would build His church "upon this rock." What is the "rock" Jesus refers to? There have been various answers given to this question. We believe the answer is Jesus Christ and is not too difficult to find. Notice first that this passage begins in verse 13 with the question, "Whom do men say that I the Son of Man am?" Jesus is the subject of conversation in the verses preceding

His statement about the rock. After the true opinion of Christ is given and the disciples are prepared in mind, Jesus states that He will build His church upon Himself, the subject of their conversation.

To make it more forceful He compares Peter, a natural leader among the apostles and a strong personality, with Himself, the foundation of His church. "Peter" and "rock" in our passage in the Greek are nearly alike. Peter is *petros* and rock is *petra*. Petros means rock, a small rock when compared to petra which means a large rock. The word petra is used sixteen times in the New Testament. There are two things we can learn by examining each passage. First it always definitely refers to something huge or the context leaves a possibility of hugeness. Secondly it is used figuratively several times of Jesus but never of Peter or anyone else. It is so huge that a house can be built on one, Matt. 7:24, 25, or a tomb can be hewn out of one which is so large the women were wondering how they would move the stone (a different word) covering the entrance into the burial place in the petra, Matt. 27:60. Concerning the places it is used in the parable of the sower and where it calls Jesus a "rock of offence" we have no exception. These contexts do not clearly reveal the rock as huge but it is a possibility. A large rock may be under the ground and in places be so near the surface that a seed falling in that place would not have enough depth to take proper root. It may even protrude slightly above the ground making it a place of offense or stumbling to some. Rom. 9:33, 1 Cor. 10:4, 1 Peter 2:8, Matt. 7:24, 25, and Luke 6:47-48 all use petra and all refer to Christ. All other passages except Matt. 16:18 are literal and do not refer to anyone. Notice also that Peter, who was prominent in our passage, evidently understood it to mean Christ and not himself for he uses the word only once and then refers to Jesus, 1 Peter 2:8.

But what does it mean when Jesus says His assembly would be built upon this rock, Himself? He is obviously speaking figuratively. Just as a good building is built on a solid foundation so the Lord's assembly must be built upon Himself. He is the foundation or authority for everything in a New Testament church. Jesus is made known in the Bible as the only perfectly reliable source, so when we follow the

Scriptures, and particularly the New Testament which deals specifically with His churches, we are built upon Him. He is the subject of all Scripture. The places that refer to the apostles and prophets as being the foundation are stating the same truth another way. It does not mention the apostles or prophets by name because as such they are not the foundation. Only in their special offices, which are to reveal Christ by writing the New Testament, are they the foundation. Everything in a New Testament church should be founded on Him as revealed in the Word. Our membership requirements, our ordinances, our gospel, our discipline, our government, etc. should all find their undergirding in Him. "What does He say about the matter?" should be the question constantly asked by a New Testament Church.

The Gates of Hell — The Lord also said that, "the gates of hell shall not prevail against" His church. Hell is used to translate more than one Greek word. Gehenna is one. It is the place of future punishment for soul and body. Hell in this passage translates the Greek word Hades which means "the unseen world." When a person dies they pass out of this world, "the seen world," into "the unseen world." Their bodies are put into the grave and their souls go into a place of torment if lost or a place of blessing if saved, in Hades. Institutions or cities can be said to go into Hades, the unseen world, that is, to die or pass out of existence, Matt. 11:23.

There are many, for example, Satan, who would like to see the Lord's church go through those gates and out of existence. They want those gates to prevail or triumph over the Lord's church and through the ages they have tried everything in their power that that kind of church might be put out of existence. The Lord promises emphatically that His kind of church will not go out of existence, "the gates of Hell shall not prevail against it."

"Church" used generically — The Lord was speaking of His church generically. Individual New Testament churches have gone out of existence but not all of them. There have always been some of that kind on earth since the Lord built the first one. Because of the Lord's promise we believe that even if historical evidence should be lacking for certain periods we can believe, and must as Christians,

28

that there have always been New Testament churches. The Lord's promise will not fail and it is better than all the historical evidence in the world. We do not believe in perpetuity of New Testament churches down to today because we can prove it historically but because the Lord taught it. During certain periods we have historical evidence which is strong for perpetuity but with our knowledge we would not contend that it is absolutely conclusive from a historian's point of view. We have proof that is much greater and is absolutely conclusive from a Christian's point of view — the Lord has promised and His word cannot fail.

The Keys of the Kingdom of Heaven — Peter was promised "the keys of the kingdom of Heaven." Other Scriptures make it plain though that it was not exclusively for him but for other members of a New Testament church also. To be a member of the Lord's kingdom is a blessing only for the saved. John 3:3 makes it plain that only the regenerate are members. The keys will open the kingdom to some and lock it to others. What are the keys? The Bible teaches that the truths about Christ must be preached. When these keys are used people are saved and admitted into the Lord's kingdom. Some people refuse this message of salvation and they are hardened, 2 Cor. 2:14-17. The use of the keys is the work of New Testament churches. Peter in himself or a New Testament church in itself cannot admit anyone into the Lord's kingdom. Only when the keys are used does this happen. The binding and loosing implies that not all will be saved when the gospel is preached. But whatever is accomplished in using the keys will have Heaven's or God's approval. The verb tense of the Greek verbs translated "bind" and "loose" is the future perfect which is rarely used. It should be correctly translated whatsoever thou shalt bind on earth "shall have been bound" in heaven and whatsoever thou shalt loose on earth "shall have been loosed" in heaven. The teaching is that whatever is accomplished by preaching the gospel has already been accomplished in heaven in God's plan. Our accomplishments by using the keys are not a surprise to God but in perfect harmony with His plan which was made before the creation of the world.

"I will build" — Jesus said, "I will build" which is the future tense. This is the usual translation of this tense

which would indicate that the church had not been built at the moment of speaking but might be at any time in the future. However it is possible to translate this tense "I will be building." There is some reason to believe that this might be the best translation here. This translation could imply that He had already begun the building of His church and would continue to build it as He gave other teachings to it. Most of the doctrines of His church had been given. There were still some to give such as His teaching concerning discipline in Matt. 18:15-20 and His teaching concerning the ordinance of the Lord's Supper in Matt. 26:26-29.

The Church began in the Lord's Personal Ministry — We would not be dogmatic on this point but we are confident that the Lord's church was founded sometime in His personal ministry even though it might be after Matt. 16. The exact time in His personal ministry we cannot say. Nearly all of the elements were present then. They had the message of salvation (Luke 9:2, 6; Mark 1:1; Matt. 24:14), the two ordinances (John 4:2; Matt. 26:26-28), the great commission (Matt. 28:19-20), people qualified to be members since they were saved and baptized (John 4:1), discipline (Matt. 18:15-20), the basic principles of church government, independence and democracy (Matt. 18:17-18; 23:8), and officers to lead the church, the apostles (Luke 6:13-16; 1 Cor. 12:28). However during His personal ministry the specific offices of pastor and deacon are not mentioned in the Gospels. They might have been mentioned though but were to be revealed later.

Hebrews 2:12 indicates that Jesus sang in the church. This would have to be during His personal ministry. The Bible indicates that Jesus sang at the giving of the Lord's Supper which may be the time referred to. Matt. 18:17 strongly implies that a church was in existence then. The apostles are said to be placed in the church, 1 Cor. 12:28. This would be more easily understood if this took place in the Lord's earthly ministry. The great commission is spoken of in such a way that it cannot be conceived that it was given to the disciples as individuals, which it would have to be, if the church was not then in existence. The Lord said He would be with them to the end of the age. The individuals died but if He was speaking to them as a church then it is being fulfilled because that kind of church still remains. Acts 1 and 2 tells of an organization of at least 120 that had a business meeting and later had 3,000 added to them on the Day of Pentecost. This group is definitely called the church of Jerusalem in Acts. We believe that the church was accredited on the day of Pentecost when it was baptized in the Holy Spirit and the miracles followed. It could not be accredited unless already in existence. We will discuss this accreditation next.

THE ACCREDITATION OF THE CHURCH

Events on the Day of Pentecost — On the day of Pentecost the church at Jerusalem, the only church of the Lord in existence, having at least 120 members were met together, Acts 1, 2. Suddenly the Holy Spirit came upon this church and they were immersed in the Holy Spirit. This had been promised by John the Baptist and the Lord. The results were a sound "as of a rushing mighty wind." "cloven tongues like as of fire" on each member, all were filled with the Holy Spirit, and all "began to speak with other tongues." These tongues were languages that they were able to speak without any previous study. Jews who spoke these languages had come to Jerusalem for the feast of Pentecost and were able to hear the message of God in their own languages. When these spectacular and miraculous events took place the Jews in Jerusalem were greatly impressed knowing that the Jews speaking were not from their countries. They were all amazed having different ideas as to the meaning of these events. Peter explained the event as a fulfillment of an Old Testament Scripture in Joel which should particularly impress these Jews and also as the work of the crucified, risen, and ascended Lord Jesus Christ.

The Purpose of the Miracles — This event was to accredit this new institution, the church, to the Jews. It was to show it was of God. The Jews saw what the church was doing and Peter explained their supernatural power as coming from Jesus Christ who was at the right hand of God the Father. God gave this institution, the church, the message of Christ to preach and gave it supernatural power to accredit it. He by-passed the temple and other divinely given institutions of the past signifying this was the institution He would work through now.

Divine Institutions in the Past Accredited — This supernatural accreditation was to be expected. God had always in the past accredited His institutions by supernatural events. Notice the beginning of the Jewish nation. The nation's leader, Moses, was accredited by miracles, Ex. 4:1-9. The giving of the law to the Jews was accredited by supernatural occurrences, Ex. 19:16-20:21. The tabernacle and temple were also accredited, Ex. 40:34-35, 1 Kings 8:10-11. God chose the Jewish people to be the channel through which His truth was to come to all. Every institution of theirs had supernatural accreditation so that none could have good reason for not accepting them as of God. The Jewish institutions such as the temple, the sacrifices, etc. had been fulfilled in Christ. God had chosen to reveal His truth by a new institution, the church. This church had been built during Jesus' personal ministry and now at Pentecost it was to be so-to-speak unveiled before the Jews and approved of God. The Jews could never be expected to accept this new institution if it were not supernaturally approved of God as their other institutions had been.

Miracles were not to Continue — Some have thought the miracles of tongues, healing, etc. were to continue and have sought to do those things, although without success. They have not understood that these supernatural events were not to continue. When God accredited His institutions in the past He did not continue the supernatural events. The unusual occurrences attending the giving of the law were not continued. Every generation did not have the law accredited. Once was enough. The accreditation of the tabernacle and temple was not continuous. We have the inspired record of these accreditations so God does not repeat them to every generation. The accreditation of the church at Jerusalem was not just for that one particular church but for every church of that kind. It is the only institution in the New Testament proclaiming the truth of God that has Divine approval.

THE MISSION WORK OF THE CHURCH

The Great Commission — Before the Lord ascended He left a work for His church to do. They were to win converts to Him by preaching the gospel. The converts were to be baptized and then taught all things. Just as the first family was commanded by God to be fruitful and multiply so the first church had the great commission which in effect said be fruitful and multiply. Baptized believers were to be the mission object of the church which could be the material for new churches of the same kind. The New Testament churches by their very mission purpose are to reproduce other New Testament churches. They are not to die or be inactive but to be fruitful and multiply. Evangelism and missions are necessary for New Testament churches. They were to begin in Jerusalem and then to carry the work to Judea, Samaria, and the uttermost parts of the world. Matt. 28:19, 20; Acts 1:8. Acts tells of the work of the Jerusalem church under the leadership of Peter in the first twelve chapters. The message is carried to Jerusalem, Judea, and Samaria in these chapters.

Persecution Spread the Gospel — Acts 8:1 tells of a great persecution of the church at Jerusalem that scatters the church into the surrounding country. This persecution greatly helped the mission work. People were saved and new churches soon were established. Saul, the great persecutor, was saved and eventually became Paul, the apostle, when the Lord appeared to him on his way to Damascus to persecute the Christians.

The Gospel was for the World — The Scriptures also reveal certain conversions that were to teach us and particularly the Jews of that day that the message of salvation was for every nation and race. Samaritans, an Ethiopian, and a Roman soldier are shown to be saved and accepted of God on an equal footing with the Jews, Acts 8, 10, 11. The Lord had taught the Jews to be a nation separate from other nations in the Old Testament for special reasons. However the necessity for that was over and so that all might know that people in all nations can be saved and be on an equal basis in a New Testament church, the Lord taught an individual lesson in Acts 10 to Peter. A sheet was let down with all kinds of unclean animals and Peter was commanded to eat. Peter balked but the Lord told him to eat. This was to prepare Peter to preach to Cornelius and to accept him on an equal basis. One purpose of the laws concerning not eating unclean animals in the Old Testament was to separate God's nation from other nations that did eat unclean animals. This separation was discontinued now as far as national lines went. Peter preached to Cornelius and his house, and God approved them as He did His church at Pentecost, showing that what Peter had done was right. Acts 10:44-48; 11:15-18.

Paul is Sent Out — The rest of Acts from 13 to 28 tells primarily of the work of the church of Antioch in sending Paul out as a missionary to the uttermost parts of the world. Acts 13:1-3 mentions that Paul and Barnabas were sent out by a church. Paul made three missionary journeys and a trip to Rome as a prisoner. Each journey was used to spread the gospel to areas around the Mediterranean Sea. Paul's practice was to win converts and then organize them into churches. The Scriptures tell of His activities in various cities and islands in the areas of Asia Minor, Macedonia, Greece, and Italy.

The Jerusalem Conference — After his first journey Paul returned to the church that sent him out to report on his work, Acts 14:26-28. There were certain Jews who believed that to be saved you must not only believe on Christ but you must also become a Jew. They taught that circumcision was necessary for salvation, Acts 15:1. This was contrary to all the teachings of Scripture, Old Testament and New Testament. The church at Antioch sent Paul and others to Jerusalem to inquire about this matter. The apostles were there and also the first church that the Lord founded. They came to discuss the matter with these men, many of whom knew the Lord in person and had been given special gifts of the Holy Spirit.

Peter and James both said that salvation was by faith in Christ alone for all, Jew and Gentile. Peter recalled his experience at Cornelius' house to back up his statements, Acts 15:7-11. James referred to the Old Testament to prove his opinion but added that the saved Gentiles should be careful of their testimony. The Gentiles did not have the background of the Jews in the laws of God and would naturally be more inclined to slip into their old life. Jews would notice any deviations in their lives. The saved Gentiles were to be careful lest they be a stumbling block to the Jews. Paul and Barnabas revealed how that God had accredited their conversions among the Gentiles by miracles, Acts 15:12. The brethren at Jerusalem then authorized the sending of letters to areas where the false teachers had gone, stating that they were not authorized by the church at Jerusalem. Their plan of salvation by works was condemned.

Other Missionaries — The missionary work of Paul was not all of the missionary work that was done. It was primarily all that God saw fit to reveal in Scripture. Other non-biblical sources indicate that the other apostles went into other areas preaching the gospel and establishing churches. The Bible reveals that the message went into all the world in this first century, Col. 1:5-6, 23. Some would interpret this to mean the Roman world or the known world. It would seem best to interpret it "the known world" which would be much wider than the Roman world.

THE OPPOSITION TO THE CHURCH

Persecution Until Paul's Conversion — The first century was a time of great persecution for the churches. The Jewish authorities were the first persecutors. It began when they took Peter and John and warned them about preaching concerning the resurrection of Jesus, Acts. 4. The apostles were imprisoned next but let out by God and then recaptured, warned not to preach Christ, beaten, and then released, Acts 5. The persecution became very strong though when certain men of one of the synagogues could not win in a dispute with Stephen. Being angry they brought him to the Jewish authorities who became infuriated when He preached a great message to them. In a rage they stoned Stephen to death. This set off a massive persecution led by Saul, Acts 6:8-8:4. Before this there had been persecution of the leaders of the church at Jerusalem but beginning at this time all of the members were persecuted. This outbreak of persecution did not stop until Saul was saved, Acts 9:31. Herod put James the son of Zebedee to death and imprisoned Peter but the Lord enabled him to escape.

Paul is Persecuted — When Saul was saved and began to preach he became the target of the Jews. He was probably hated so much because he had been a leader in the persecution of the Christians and then joined them. On his missionary journeys he met with great persecution. Much of this was from the Jews also. In his first missionary journey some of the Jews persecuted him and stirred up some of the Gentiles to join them. Because of some Jews Paul and Barnabas were put out of cities and Paul was stoned.

On Paul's second missionary journey he received persecution from Gentiles. When an evil spirit had been cast out of a woman certain men became angry at Paul and stirred up a persecution against him and Silas. Their means of making money was cut off so they persecuted. At Ephesus the salvation of many hurt the idol making business and this resulted in persecution. In general some Jews persecuted Paul everywhere he went. He finally was imprisoned by them in Jerusalem and then in Caesarea where he appealed to Caesar and was taken to Rome for trial. Eventually he was executed in Rome. The other apostles and Christians suffered also.

Roman Persecution — During the first century the persecution of Christians was usually by certain Jews. Roman persecution was local and intermittent. Nero (54-68 A. D.) put Paul to death and brutally killed the Christians. He blamed them for the burning of Rome to shift the blame from himself. Domitian (81-96 A. D.), the Roman emperor, persecuted those who would not worship the emperor. This persecution was against anyone guilty. Christians would not obey and suffered.

Heresy During New Testament Days — There was not only outward opposition to New Testament churches in this century but also inward opposition. The inward opposition came from professed Christians that sought to change the doctrines set down by the Lord. We have already seen that some tried to make circumcision necessary for salvation, Acts 15. Paul warned and denounced those that would try to change the gospel to salvation by works, Gal. 1:6-9. Some denied the true Deity of Christ and some His true humanity. The Lord's Supper was perverted by the Corinthian church, 1 Cor. 11. The bodily resurrection was denied by some. These and other heresies existed in the first century. There was a constant battle to correct heresy within the churches. Despite these heresies everything indicates that as a whole the churches of the first century remained sound in the faith.

The Period Of Apostasy: 100-313

THE PERSECUTION OF THE NEW TESTAMENT CHURCHES

Introduction — The churches of the first century are not given any special name for there was only one kind of Christian church. We have noticed their doctrines and have found that they were identical with the churches now called Baptist churches. These New Testament churches and the heresies that were beginning to develop in some of them continued on into this period. The heresies that were only in miniature in the first century became practically full-grown by the end of this period with many adherents. The development of heresy dominated this time and gives the period its name. A new kind of church had come into existence by the end of the period and names are needed to distinguish one from another.

The Roman Citizen's Attitude Toward Christians — We will first notice the true churches briefly. They began the period as the only kind of Christian churches in existence. They ended the period by going into obscurity and another kind of church becoming dominant. The true churches retained their beliefs and practices with which we are familiar. It was their persecution by the Roman Empire that we should notice. Not only did the government persecute at times but there was a great hatred manifested for the Christians by the common people and by the intellectual people. The people did not understand their beliefs and drew false conclusions about them from the few facts known. Christians were accused of being cannibals because they ate the bread and drank the wine of the Lord's Supper, spoken of as the Lord's body and blood, their accusers not understanding that this was not literal. The pagans as a whole could not conceive of God apart from idols and since the Christians had none they were atheists.

Christians spoke of their love for their brethren and sisters in Christ and since the common people of the day knew only of a sensual love they misunderstood the Christians and considered them immoral. The Christians separated themselves from the brutal and immoral shows such as the gladiator contests of the day and also lived lives that were contrary to the standards of the day for which they were hated. The Christian religion if spread would have hurt the businesses of the idol makers and others that did some work connected with the pagan religions. This also brought hatred upon them. Whenever any catastrophes occurred such as earthquakes, floods, etc. the superstitious people were certain that their gods must be offended. The reason they thought for the anger of the gods must be the beliefs and practices of the Christians which were contrary to their heathen religions. The intellectuals of the day attacked in writing the beliefs and practices of the Christians. The supernatural events of the Bible were considered as impossible and were treated with scorn. The doctrines of Christ, salvation, etc. were not understood and so they were attacked.

The Roman Government's Attitude Toward Christians — The Roman government in the early years of the second century established a policy that was followed the rest of that century and well into the third century. The Christian religion was contrary to the Roman religion but it was considered harmless. Christians would not be bothered unless responsible men wanted action taken against them. When such action was desired the Christians tried were commanded to deny the Christian faith or suffer death. Even though many suffered and died during this period persecution was not found everywhere in the Roman Empire. Neither was it continuous. The first universal attempt to exterminate Christianity began in 250 and continued about ten years. The Roman Empire was declining and one theory for the decline was that the gods were offended with the empire because of the Christians. Some felt that the glory of Rome could be restored by destroying Christianity so the Emperor Decius started the persecution against every Christian. Many Christians were tortured and killed. Some professed Christians compromised to save their lives. The persecution let up when it was seen that the Empire continued to decline. For similar reasons the Emperor Diocletian began a universal persecution in 305 in which many Christians died. A few years after this universal persecution Constantine came to power and favored the Christians. This ended persecution by the pagan Roman Empire. The worst calamity that overtook the Christians during this period was not the terrible persecution from without but the gradual change of doctrine within some of the churches. The opposition without could not destroy them. The heresy within was the most destructive force. Many churches were to fall as a result of heresy and that is the story we want to consider now.

THE DEVELOPMENT OF THE APOSTATE CHURCHES

Heresy on Baptism — During this period the ordinances were changed in some churches. Baptism was considered to be more than symbolic. Some thought that it was necessary to salvation. Regeneration was thought to take place when one was baptized. Immersion was the mode with few exceptions all during this period. The ordinary mode was immersion for centuries. Some historians believe infant baptism began during this period while others believe its beginning was a little later. There are a few statements that indicate that it may have begun towards the close of this period. When it was taught that baptism regenerated, infant baptism became inevitable. It was just a matter of time.

Heresy on the Lord's Supper — The Lord's Supper was not changed as to its elements or as to who should participate but it was changed in its meaning. It was considered more than symbolic. The elements were thought to be changed in some mystical way after it was consecrated and they conveyed grace to the ones participating. The observance of the Lord's Supper became the main part of the service rather than preaching. The service began to be called the "mass" which comes from a Latin word meaning "dismissal." It received this name because those who were not eligible to partake of the supper were asked to leave. The next step was inevitable and there were indications that it was already in the minds of some. The Lord's Supper was considered a repetition of the offering of Christ on the cross. The changing of the meaning of the two ordinances resulted in changes in the plan of salvation, church membership, and the work of a pastor.

Other Heresies — The plan of salvation was no longer by grace through faith in Christ as taught in the Bible. Faith and grace were terms still used but their meanings were changing to fit new ideas. Baptism was necessary for salvation and other things were being added as also necessary. Salvation was by human efforts according to these churches.

Church membership was different also. Since salvation and baptism were different it could not help but be so. Baptism was not administered after a person professed faith in Christ but after a long period of instruction. The pastor or elder began to be called priest during this period and there was a shift from an emphasis on preaching to performing the rituals just exactly right. The mass must be performed in just a certain way. The services became very mystical and ritualistic. In making these changes the Bible had to be misinterpreted, contradicted, and at times entirely put aside in favor of some new authority. The Bible was no longer the final rule of faith and practice for the apostate churches.

Relics — The bones of the saints, the sign of the cross, special days, religious relics and religious processions began to have special sanctity. These externals came to have a large part in the religious life of some. Mary was also given adoration unbefitting any one but God.

Heresy on Church Government — Another major change during this period was in the governments of some churches. Pastors of certain large churches obtained control over the smaller surrounding churches and the pastors of these smaller churches were called presbyters, meaning elders. In time they were called priests. The pastors of the large churches were called bishops meaning overseers. In the New Testament bishop and presbyter were titles given to the same office. This office was what Baptists today refer to as pastor. It was an office of a local church; it was not an office over several churches. Each church was self-governing in the New Testament. This change brought into being a new office that was greater than any previous office connected with New Testament churches but using a term from the New Testament to designate it. These churches were no longer independent and self-governing. The bishop of the area was over the priests of the surrounding churches and he also had the power over the people in the churches. The bishop controlled the ordinances that were believed to have saving value, baptism and the Lord's Supper. He alone could authorize these ordinances or sacraments as they began to be called. This gave him power over everybody in these churches for they believed these sacraments were necessary for salvation. The bishops of the larger cities in time took special titles such as archbishop or patriarch to elevate themselves above the bishops of the smaller cities.

Conclusion — These changes were not to be fixed but only the foundation for other changes in the next period. All of the essential elements for the Roman Catholic Church were developed though. The next period will see these elements further developed and the bishop of the Roman Church will take control of the apostate churches of the western Roman Empire.

The Period Of Obscurity: 313-1638

THE APOSTATE CHURCHES RISE TO POWER

Constantine and Christianity — This period began with the rise to power of the Emperor Constantine and his favoring of Christianity. In 305 Diocletian, the Emperor, had sought to destroy Christianity thinking this was the way to save the declining empire. Shortly after this Constantine came to power and sought to use Christianity to save the empire. They could not destroy it so they tried using it.

Constantine claimed to have seen a vision of a flaming cross in the sky with the words, "By this conquer," before an important battle which he won. He professed Christianity and favored it by laws. In 313 Christians were given freedom of worship but it was not adopted as the official and exclusive religion of the state until 395, long after Constantine's time. During these years it was favored more and more by the state with the exception of the years of the reign of Julian, the Apostate.

Constantine was converted to the teachings of the apostate churches. His life did not show the fruits of a Christian. In fact he waited until a few days before his death to be baptized so that all of his sins might be washed away in that rite. Constantine's acceptance of Christianity was to have a tremendous effect upon the true churches and the apostate churches.

The Apostate Churches are Favored by the Governments — The apostate churches received the favor of the Roman state at this time and continued to be closely connected with the governments of Europe until the Reformation period when some governments favored the reformation churches. At times these churches and the state were on better terms with each other than at other times. At times this church dominated and at other times it was the state that dominated.

The Roman Catholic Church Begins — It was during this period that the apostate churches developed into what is now called the Roman Catholic church and the Greek Catholic church. The bishops of Rome claimed to have the supremacy over the other churches from time to time. This claim was generally recognized in the western Roman Empire by the time Leo I came to the head of the Roman church in 440. It is difficult to point to the time that the Roman Catholic Church began since it was a gradual growth of error but many point to 440 as the time that the apostate churches of the west generally admitted Rome's supremacy. Some would claim the beginning to be with Pope Gregory I in 590. We think 440 is the best date.

The Apostate Churches in the East — The churches of the east had several bishops that sought to be the head but the Bishop of Constantinople was able to win out. The moving of the headquarters of the Roman Empire to that city helped him to his power but also prevented him from ever having the power of the Roman Bishop. The bishop was overshadowed by the Emperor being in the same city. The Roman Bishop and the Bishop of Constantinople had a contest for centuries for supremacy, neither ever winning a decisive victory. The two churches split in 1054 and have gone their separate ways ever since then.

The Apostate Churches Persecute the New Testament Churches — Constantine's professed conversion also had a great effect upon the New Testament churches. The apostate churches that were favored and closely connected with the state from this time on persecuted the true churches as heretics. The churches that had accepted the heretical teachings were known as orthodox and true churches since they were in power. The churches that were true to the New Testament teachings were now considered heretics. Often, even in the writings of non-catholic historians, what they describe as the New Testament churches in the first century are spoken of as heresies in the fourth century and later. The New Testament churches had been persecuted by the Jews and the Roman government for the first three centuries but starting in this century they are persecuted for centuries by the apostate churches and the governments with which they were united.

THE HISTORICAL EVIDENCE FOR NEW TESTAMENT CHURCHES IN THIS PERIOD

New Testament Churches Called by Various Names — The Baptists go into obscurity during this period. At times the Roman and Eastern Catholic churches so dominate the scenes that it seems that no other kind of church exists. But they do exist because God's Word promises that they will and there is historical evidence to support this promise.

During this period the churches that existed outside of the Roman Catholic churches were called by various names. They often received their names because of some outstanding leader or some characteristic. The information concerning them is small and often written by their enemies. Their enemies didn't understand their beliefs and usually wrote from a very prejudiced viewpoint. Much of the information available tells of their persecution. Few documents are available that tell of their beliefs and practices written from their point of view.

Not every group outside of the Catholics were New Testament churches. Some though give every indication that they would be called Baptists today. Many Baptist historians have written stating that they believed these groups were Baptists. Some Baptist historians have been very cautious and have not claimed these groups as definitely Baptist but only as holding some Baptist principles.

The Petrobrusians — We do not claim that we can prove that each of these groups are definitely Baptists from the historical evidence available. We believe some can be proved to be Baptists though and others seem to be Baptists from the information available but we would need more information to definitely prove it. We would like to notice several groups as examples of what we find in this period. The Petrobrusian churches are found in Southern France around 1100. They received their name from one of their great leaders, Peter of Bruys. H. C. Vedder, one of the most cautious of Baptist historians, after examining what one of their enemies claimed were their errors says,

> It is evident that the "errors" of the Petrobrusians were what Baptist have always maintained to be the fundamental truths of the Scriptures. Any body of Christians that holds to the supremacy of the Scriptures, a church of the regenerate only, and believers' baptism, is

fundamentally one with the Baptist churches of today, whatever else it may add to or omit from its statement of beliefs. Contemporary records have been sought in vain to establish any essential doctrine taught by this condemned sect that is inconsistent either with the teaching of Scripture or with the beliefs avowed in recent times by Baptists. [H. C. Vedder, *A Short History of the Baptists*, p. 115.]

The Paulicians — Another group that is found from the seventh century to the reformation are the Paulicians. The enemies of the Paulicians in writing against them stated that they were Manichaeans and that they denied the ordinances. Even though many historians questioned these statements and believed the Paulicians to be misrepresented, they had no real historical evidence to support what they thought was the true character of these churches. Some encyclopedias and histories of less than one hundred years ago accepted these charges against the Paulicians as fact having nothing better than the accounts of their enemies to go by. If they were Manichaeans and did not practice the ordinances of course they could not be Baptists. Some scholars suspected though that they were not Manichaeans and that the Greek Catholics writing against them did not understand them or were willfully misrepresenting them. They thought that since the Paulicians probably condemned the ordinances as practiced by the Catholics, the Catholic writers, believing their observance of the ordinances to be the only true observance, stated that the Paulicians denied the ordinances. The ordinances as practiced by the Paulicians would of course not be recognized by the Catholics. These suspicions were proved to be true when other historical data was uncovered around the beginning of the twentieth century which dated back to the middle ages. Some of this new material was written by Paulicians stating their beliefs. This material proved definitely that they did observe both ordinances. They believed that only believers in Christ were subjects for baptism denying strongly infant baptism and the baptism as observed by the Catholics. They practiced baptism by immersion and appealed to the Scriptures for the authority of their beliefs. Similar statements have been made against other groups by their enemies. Some scholars have reason to doubt these accusations but lack the historical evidence to prove conclusively what they think is the real character of these groups. This example concerning the Paulician history should warn us of the statements made by the enemies of other groups.

The Bogomils — Dr. L. P. Brockett's conclusions about the Bogomils are quoted by Dr. J. T. Christian in his history.

> Among these (historians of the Bulgarians) I have found, often in unexpected quarters, the most conclusive evidence that these sects were all, during their early history, Baptists, not only in their views on the subjects of baptism and the Lord's Supper, but in their opposition to Pedobaptism, to a church hierarchy, and to the worship of the virgin Mary and the saints, and in their adherence to church independency and freedom of conscience in religious worship. In short, the conclusion has forced itself upon me that in these Christians of Bosnia, Bulgaria, and Armenia we have an apostolic succession of Christian churches, New Testament churches, and that as early as the twelfth century these churches numbered a converted, believing membership, as large as that of the Baptist churches throughout the world today (Brockett, the Bogomils of Bulgaria and Bosnia, 11, 12). [J. T. Christian, *A History of the Baptists*, Vol. I, p. 58.]

The Beginning of the Waldenses — A better known group during this time was the Waldenses. We believe the evidence coming from the twelfth century proves that they were Baptists. The Waldenses claimed to go back to the first century. Some historians believe this to be true while others think they began with Peter Waldo. Peter Waldo was a great preacher among them but not their founder. Broadbent says,

> In the Alpine valleys of Piedmont there had been for centuries congregations of believers calling themselves brethren, who came later to be widely known as Waldenses, or Vaudois, though they did not themselves accept the name. They traced their origin in those parts back to Apostolic times. Like many of the so-called Cathar, Paulician, and other churches, these were not 'reformed' never having degenerated from the New Testament pattern as had the Roman, Greek, and some others, but having always maintained, in varying degree,

the Apostolic tradition. From the time of Constantine
there had continued to be a succession of those who
preached the Gospel and founded churches, uninfluenced
by the relations between church and state existing at the
time. This accounts for the large bodies of Christians, well
established in the Scriptures and free from idolatry and the
other evils prevailing in the dominant, professing church, to
be found in the Taurus Mountains and Alpine valleys.
[E. H. Broadbent, *The Pilgrim Church*, pp. 89, 90.

The Doctrine of the Waldenses — The historical
evidence shows that they held to the Bible as the final
authority for faith and practice and that salvation was
wholly of grace through faith in Christ as Savior. They also
believed that the ordinances were only baptism and the
Lord's supper and they were only symbolic, that only
believers should be baptized, that baptism was by
immersion, and that salvation and baptism were the
requirements for church membership.

A Waldensian confession of faith of the year 1120
states:

> We do believe that the sacraments are signs of the
> holy thing, or visible forms of invisible grace accounting it
> good that the faithful sometimes use the said signs or
> visible forms, if it may be done. However, we believe and
> hold, that the above-said faithful may be saved without
> receiving the signs aforesaid, in case they have no place
> nor any means to use them. We acknowledge no other
> sacrament but baptism and the Lord's Supper. [Samuel
> Morland, *The Churches of the Valley of Piedmont*, p. 34.]

Today Baptists refrain from ordinarily using the word
"sacrament" to refer to Baptism and the Lord's Supper
because usually when it is used by others it carries the idea
that these rites have some saving value. We prefer the word
"ordinance" since it carries no such connections. However,
the way the Waldenses used the word "sacrament" here
shows that they intended to mean no more than what we
mean by "ordinance." The context clearly shows that they
connect no saving value with it. In another confession of
faith of 1544 they say,

> We believe that in the ordinance of baptism the
> water is the visible and external sign, which represents to

us that which, by virtue of God's invisible operation, is
within us, the renovation of our minds, and the
mortification of our members through (the faith of) Jesus
Christ. And by this ordinance we are received into the
holy congregation of God's people, previously professing
our faith and the change of life (Sleiden, The General
History of the Reformation, 347. London, 1689). [J. T.
Christian, *Op. Cit.*, p. 78.]

They immersed their converts. Christian says,

Eberhard and Ermengard, in their work "contra
Waldenses," written toward the close of the twelfth
century, repeatedly refer to immersion as the form of
baptism among the Waldenses. [*Op. Cit.*, pp. 81-82.]

They rejected infant baptism and were condemned by
their enemies for it. Christian states,

It is possible that some of the Italian Waldenses
(so-called) practiced infant baptism (Dollinger,
Sektengeschichte, II, 52). There is no account that the
French Waldenses, or the Waldenses proper, ever practiced
infant baptism. [*Op. Cit.*, p. 77.]

Broadbent indicates from the following quotation that
they were democratic and self-governing.

In matters of discipline, appointment of elders, and
other acts, the whole church took part in conjunction with
its elders. [E. H. Broadbent, *Op. Cit.*, p. 99.]

The Waldenses in Later Times — It is sometimes
objected that the Waldenses of the reformation period and
today do not hold to these views. It is true that some of
their churches changed about the time of the reformation
but the Waldenses before this believed as a whole as we
have stated. Historical documents confirm this.

In the face of all but unanimous testimony of
Roman authorities, it has been denied that the early
Waldenses rejected infant baptism. Stress is laid on the fact
that in the earliest of their literature that has come down
to us the Waldensians are Pedobaptists, or at least do not
oppose infant baptism. It is also an unquestioned fact that
the later Waldensians — those who found a refuge in the
valleys of Savoy after the crusade of Simon de Montfort in

Southern France — are found to be Pedobaptists at the earliest authentic period of their history. But all this is not necessarily inconsistent with the accounts of the sect as given us by contemporary Romanists. Nearly three hundred years elapsed between the crusade and the Reformation, and during these centuries the escaped Waldenses dwelt among the high valleys of Eastern France and Savoy, isolated and forgotten. Great ignorance came upon them, as is testified by the literature that has survived, and in time they so far forgot the doctrines of their forefathers that many of the writers saw but little difference between themselves and the Romanists. Some of the old spirit remained, however, so that when in 1532 a Pedobaptist creed was adopted at the Synod of Angrogne, under the guidance of the Swiss reformers, Farel and OEcolampadius, a large minority refused to be bound by this new creed, declaring it to be a reversal of their previous beliefs. That they were correct in this interpretation is the verdict of modern scholars who have thoroughly investigated the earlier Waldensian history.

The balance of evidence is therefore clearly in favor of the conclusion that the early followers of Waldo taught and practiced the baptism of believers only. Dr. Keller, the latest and most candid investigator of the subject, holds this view: 'Very many Waldenses considered, as we know accurately, the baptism on (profession of) faith to be that form which is conformable with the words and example of Christ. They held this to be the sign of the covenant of a good conscience with God, and it was certain to them that it had value only as such.' This belief would logically exclude infant baptism, and accordingly Dr. Keller tells us, 'Mostly they let their children be baptized (by Romish priests?), yet with the reservation that this ceremony was null and void.' Maintaining these views, they were the spiritual ancestors of the Anabaptist churches that sprang up all over continental Europe in the early years of the Reformation. [H. C. Vedder, *Op. Cit.*, p. 82.]

Dr. Christian says,

Every institution has its vicissitudes, and after progress comes decline. On the eve of the Reformation everything was on the decline — faith, life, light. It was so of the Waldenses. Persecution had wasted their numbers and had broken their spirit and the few scattered leaders were dazed by the rising glories of the Reformation. The larger portion had gone with the Anabaptist movement. Sick and tired of heart in 1530 the remnant of the Waldenses opened negotiations with the Reformers, but a union was not effected till 1532. Since then the Waldenses have been Pedobaptists. [J. T. Christian, *Op. Cit.*, p. 82.]

The Anabaptists Introduced — We would now like to consider the Anabaptists. This is a very old name going back to the third century. The term "anabaptist" means re-baptizer. It has been used to designate a number of groups holding to different doctrines. Some of these groups were not Baptists but others were. There was a fanatical group at Munster in Germany that sought to set up the millennial kingdom of Christ. They were called Anabaptists but they were quite different in doctrine from the vast majority of people called Anabaptists. This group at Munster were not Baptists and many scholars have admitted this.

The Anabaptists and Earlier New Testament Churches — Vedder makes an interesting observation concerning the connection between the Anabaptists of the reformation period and Baptist groups prior to that time.

> And it is a curious and instructive fact that the Anabaptist churches of the Reformation period were most numerous precisely where the Waldenses of a century or two previous had most flourished, and where their identity as Waldenses had been lost. That there was an intimate relation between the two movements, few doubt who have studied this period and its literature. The torch of truth was handed on from generation to generation, and though it often smoldered and was even apparently extinguished, it needed but a breath to blaze up again and give light to all mankind. [H. C. Vedder, *Op. Cit.*, p. 128.]

Vedder continues.

> The utmost that can be said in the present state of historical research is that a moral certainty exists of a connection between the Swiss Anabaptists and their Waldensian and Petrobrusian predecessors, sustained by many significant facts, but not absolutely proved by historical evidence. Those who maintain that the Anabaptists originated with the Reformation have some difficult problems to solve, among others the rapidity with which the new leaven spread, and the wide territory that the Anabaptists so soon covered. It is common to regard them as an insignificant handful of fanatics, but abundant documentary proofs exist to show that they were numerous, widespread, and indefatigable; that their chief men were not inferior in learning and eloquence to any of

the reformers; that their teachings were scriptural, consistent, and moderate, except where persecution produced the usual result of enthusiasm and vagary.

Another problem demanding solution is furnished by the fact that these Anabaptist churches were not gradually developed, but appear fully formed from the first — complete in polity, sound in doctrine, strict in discipline. It will be found impossible to account for these phenomena without an assumption of a long-existing cause. Though the Anabaptist churches appear suddenly in the records of the time, contemporaneously with the Zwinglian Reformation, their roots are to be sought farther back. [*Op. Cit.*, p. 130.]

The Doctrines of The Anabaptists — There was a great group of churches called Anabaptists that held to the distinctives of the Baptists. Here we would like to quote excerpts from a confession of faith of some Swiss Anabaptists dated before 1527.

Baptism should be given to all those who have learned repentance and change of life, and believe in truth that their sins have been taken away through Christ; and to all those who desire to walk in the resurrection of Jesus Christ, and to be buried with Him in death, that with Him they may rise, and to all those who with such intention themselves desire and request it of us. By this is excluded all infant baptism, the Pope's highest and first abomination . . . Excommunication should be pronounced on all those who have given themselves to the Lord, to walk in His commandments, and on all those who have been baptized into one body of Christ, and who call themselves brothers and sisters, and yet slip away and fall into sin and are overtaken unawares. They should be warned the second time privately, and the third time publicly rebuked before the whole congregation, or be excluded according to the command of Christ, Matt. 18. But this should take place, according to the order of the Spirit of God, before the breaking of bread, that we may with one mind and with one love break and eat of one bread and drink of one cup . . .

All who would break one bread for a memorial of the broken body of Christ, and all who would drink one draught as a memorial of the poured out blood of Christ, should beforehand be united to one body of Christ: that is, to the Church of God, of which the head is Christ, to wit, by baptism . . .

The pastor in the congregation should be one in entire accordance with the direction of Paul, who has a good report from those who are without the faith. His office should be to read, exhort, and teach; to warn, reprove, excommunicate in the congregation, and to lead in prayer for the bettering of all brethren and sister; to take the bread, to break it, and in all things to care for the body of Christ, that it be edified and bettered, and that the mouth of the blasphemer be stopped. But he, when he is in want, must be supported by the congregation which elected him, so that he who serves the Gospel should also live from it, as the Lord has ordained. [Thomas Armitage, *A History of the Baptists*, 962-963.]

A careful reading of this indicates that they held to the Baptist distinctives concerning salvation, baptism, the Lord's Supper, church membership, and church government. They also held that the Bible was the final authority in faith and practice. We would call these churches Baptist today.

It is sometimes objected that some of these Anabaptists also believed that the taking of oaths was wrong along with other doctrines that most Baptists of today do not consider wrong. Since that is true, they say, how can you consider them Baptists? Certain groups of Baptists at times have differed on such matters. We answer that differences like these have no bearing on whether you are a Baptist or not. Baptist churches in seventeenth and eighteenth century England differed on such matters and no one says that they aren't Baptists. Some Baptists in England believed strongly that singing was wrong in the church while others thought differently.

It is also objected that Anabaptists sprinkled for baptism so they were not Baptists. This is a false statement. The fact is that some churches that were called Anabaptists did sprinkle but only some. Many churches that were Anabaptist immersed only. We claim that the Anabaptist churches holding to our distinctives were Baptists. We do not believe that the churches that were called Anabaptists that did not hold these distinctives were Baptists anymore than real Baptists today will recognize churches under the name Baptist who have begun to accept sprinkling as baptism and practice other heresies.

The Baptists and the Reformers — The Corruption of the Roman Catholic Church caused some within it to revolt. Luther, Calvin, and others were Roman Catholics who saw much of the error in their church and sought to reform it. Their efforts were of no avail so they eventually came out of the Catholic Church and formed the major Protestant churches. The Baptists were glad that the Catholic reformers were coming to Biblical truths but were also sad that they did not accept the truths concerning religious liberty, the church, its ordinances, its government, etc. The Baptists were persecuted by Catholics and Protestants during the Reformation Period. Sometimes people refer to Baptists as Protestants but this is incorrect since they had come down from the first century whereas the Protestants originated in the reformation of the sixteenth century.

Persecution of The Anabaptists — The Baptists suffered greatly during the Reformation period as they had during the many previous centuries of their existence. We cannot take the space to describe the terrible sufferings they went through. We only want to give one quotation as an example of what they went through and how they took it. Vedder quotes a Roman Catholic by the name of Cornelius which we repeat.

> In Tyrol and Gorz, the number of the executions in the year 1531 already reached one thousand; in Ensisheim, six hundred. At Linz, seventy-three were killed in six weeks. Duke William, of Bavaria, surpassing all others, issued the fearful decree to behead those who recanted, to burn those who refused to recant. Throughout the greater part of upper Germany the persecutions raged like a wild chase. The blood of these poor people flowed like water; so that they cried to the Lord for help. But hundreds of them, of all ages and both sexes, suffered the pangs of torture without a murmur, despised to buy their lives by recantation, and went to the place of execution joyful and singing Psalms. [H. C. Vedder, *Op. Cit.*, p. 165.]

Both Protestants and Roman Catholics persecuted the Baptists during this period. After the fanatical uprising in Munster which the Baptists deplored as much as anyone, all people called by the term "Anabaptist" suffered. The Anabaptists that were Baptists were not guilty of this uprising but they suffered for it. After this the Anabaptists seemed to disappear but only in appearance. Vedder says,

> But the student of history is not long in discovering

that the Anabaptists did not disappear; they only took a different name. They had never chosen the name Anabaptist, and had always maintained that it was not properly applied to them. Now that the name had come to be a synonym for all that was fanatical in creed and immoral in conduct, they were only too glad to be rid of the hateful title — as hateful to them as to their oppressors. As before, so now and after, these people called themselves simply "the brethren," but in common speech a new name came to be applied to them about the middle of the sixteenth century; they were known as Mennonites. [*Op. Cit.*, p. 184.]

Some of these churches called Mennonites in this period were Baptists in doctrine, others were not.

The Period Of Toleration: 1638-1960

THE TRANSITION

Few Historical Documents in Early Baptist History — For centuries before this period the history of Baptists is obscure. The apostate churches were closely connected with the governments of Europe and had the power. They used this power to persecute and destroy all those that differed with them, Because of this the necessary historical data to write a complete history of the Baptists for that period is not available. They do however come into view here and there at various times in the writings of their bitterest enemies. A continuous history of the churches, outstanding men, and accomplishments in that period though is impossible. Few of their own writings have been handed down. Their history is fragmentary. Since they were persecuted and condemned by their enemies, this part of their history dominates in the documents we have concerning them. The history of that period might be best designated as a martyrology.

Many Documents in Modern Times — This new period is quite different. Many documents of the Baptists are available to write a continuous history. Some of the Baptist churches of seventeenth century England are still with us. We have a list of their pastors, and their deeds. Church minutes have been preserved and many of the writings of the Baptists are still in existence. With this type of material we can write a proper history. In this period the Baptist churches come out of obscurity. The reason that so much material is available in this period to write a history is due to the coming of toleration. In 1689 religious toleration came permanently to England. Even before this there was a certain amount of toleration granted for short periods during the time of the English civil war and commonwealth. During the fifty years before the toleration act of 1689 there was much persecution of the Baptists but it was not as severe as it had been in the previous centuries. We have historical data from these fifty years because it wasn't as severe and because many Baptists of this time lived to see toleration and to bring the facts of their history with them into this new period.

English Baptists and Baptists of Former Times — In the middle years of the seventeenth. century a number of Baptist churches came into historical view. We know how some began but of others we haven't any certain knowledge. The connection of these churches with the Baptists of the past period is not absolutely clear. They are the same in doctrine though and we believe that if all the facts were available we would find a definite connection. There is evidence of groups in England and on the continent of Europe holding to Baptist distinctives in the preceding centuries.

John Smyth — Some have sought to start the Baptists with John Smyth but an examination of the facts reveals that this is not correct. He graduated from Cambridge and became a minister of the Church of England. Through his studies of the Scriptures he was led to leave the Church of England and unite with a separatist church at Gainsborough. Persecution drove Smyth and the church to seek refuge in Holland. Here he became convinced that infant baptism was wrong. He baptized himself and then the whole church. Later he believed he had made a mistake in not having the proper authority in baptizing himself and his congregation. When he told the congregation his thoughts on the matter some agreed with him but not all. The part of the church that disagreed with him separated from him and eventually returned to England under the leadership of Thomas Helwys in 1611 or 1612. Smyth and the rest of the Church stayed in Holland where they sought to join the Mennonites by baptism believing they had the proper authority. Smyth died in 1612 before being baptized into the Mennonites.

Baptists did not come from Smyth — Historians disagree on whether Smyth was affused or immersed and whether the Baptists began with him or not. It seems certain that he was immersed from the facts and there can be no question that he did not begin the Baptists. Christian, a very capable modern Baptist historian, has this to say on the subject.

> It may be of moment to remark that the baptism of
> Smyth did not affect the baptism of the Baptist churches
> of England. It has been affirmed that the General Baptist
> churches of England originated with this church of
> Smyth's; that this was the mother church of Baptists; and
> even that the Baptist denomination originated here in the
> year 1609. After prolonged investigation, we are unable to
> find the evidence that any Baptist church grew out of this
> one. We are to find that after Helwys settled with this
> church in London, some churches affiliated with it in a
> certain correspondence with some Mennonites in Holland;
> but that they had a common origin is nowhere manifest. If
> such proof exists it has escaped our attention.
> The Baptist historians of England are singularly
> unanimous on this point. 'If he (Smyth) were guilty of
> what they charge him with,' says Crosby, 'tis no blemish
> on the English Baptists; who neither approved any such
> method, nor did they receive their baptism from him'
> (Crosby, History of the English, I. 99). [J. T. Christian,
> Op. Cit., p. 225.]

Crosby's statement should be considered carefully as he wrote in the next century in England.

The Beginning of Two Particular Baptist Churches — We have records of two Baptist churches beginning in the thirties. Both churches began with people who had withdrawn from a separatist church in London called Jacob's church. These people had withdrawn and formed Baptist churches when they became convinced that only believer's baptism was Scriptural. These two churches differed on how to begin a church. One church believed that they had a right to baptize without going to any other church for authority. They used the case of John the Baptist as their reason for such a practice. This church was pastored by John Spilsbury. The other church believed that they should have the authority of some other New Testament church for their baptism so they sent Richard Blount to be baptized by a Mennonite church in Holland. He returned and baptized the other people and a church was formed. We believe that there were other New Testament churches in England that they might have sought for baptism but in those days of persecution it was not easy to learn of their whereabouts especially for people that had just come to Baptist beliefs. We mention these two churches because some historians have said that they were the first Particular Baptist churches. We would have to disagree with such an idea. We have the beginning of two churches but not the beginning of the Particular Baptist churches.

Seven Particular Baptist churches in London joined together in issuing a confession in 1644. Christian says concerning them,

> But some of the Particular Baptist Churches originated in the Independent church of Henry Jacob. There is no proof that all of the seven Particular Baptist churches of London originated in this manner. 'The Seven Churches of London, however,' says Cutting, 'are not to be supposed as comprizing the whole of the Particular Baptist denomination at that time. There were certainly several churches besides these, and their increase at a period immediately succeeding was very rapid.' [*Op. Cit.*, p. 250.]

Baptists did not begin in the 17th Century — Efforts to show that the Baptists began in England in the seventeenth century have failed. We have historical evidence of the beginning of several Baptist churches at this time but not evidence of the beginning of the first Baptist church. It would not be scholarly from a historical point of view to state that we have definite historical evidence of a connection between the Baptists of seventeenth century England and the Baptists of previous centuries. Neither is it scholarly from a historical point of view to state that Baptists began with this church or that church in the seventeenth century when we have churches of that period that we do not know how they began. We also have churches of other centuries that were Baptists as we have seen. Many more facts are needed before such a statement can be truthfully made. Such statements may please some who dislike Baptist beliefs but they are not warranted by the known facts of history.

It is our desire to relate the facts of history accurately and not to draw any conclusions that are not fully justified from the historical data available. For this reason we have been very cautious in making statements in this book. We say that historically we cannot positively show the connections between the Baptist groups in the various

58

preceeding centuries with the evidence available to our knowledge.

We do believe though that we have a continuous history back to the days of the first century but it rests upon better than historical evidence. This belief rests upon the promise of the Lord Jesus Christ in Matt. 16:18 and in other Scriptures. The historical evidence available though does help considerably to justify our belief in the Lord's promise.

It would be well to note that some Baptists of the seventeenth and eighteenth century in England believed that their history went back to Christ. If they began in the seventeenth century one would think they would know. In the seventeenth century the enemies of Baptists often called them Anabaptists which would seem to indicate that they connected them with a group going back farther than that century. Crosby and other old Baptist historians do not believe we began in the seventeenth century. We believe the testimony of men living so near this time should have some weight.

Non-Baptists Testify to Baptist Perpetuity — It should also be carefully noted that some historians of other denominations do not believe that the Baptists began in the seventeenth century but are much older. Christian writes concerning a Roman Catholic Cardinal:

> Cardinal Hosius, a member of the Council of Trent, A. D. 1560, in a statement often quoted, says:
> If the truth of religion were to be judged by the readiness and boldness of which a man of any sect shows in suffering, then the opinion and persuasion of no sect can be truer and surer than that of the Anabaptists since there have been none for these twelve hundred years past that have been more generally punished or that have more cheerfully and steadfastly undergone, and even offered themselves to the most cruel sorts of punishment than these people (Hosius, Letters Apud Opera, 112-113. Baptist Magazine CVIII, 278. May, 1826).
> That Cardinal Hosius dated the history of the Baptists back twelve hundred years, I. e. 360, is manifest, for in yet another place the Cardinal says:
> The Anabaptists are a pernicious sect. Of which kind the Waldensian brethren seem to have been, although some of them lately, as they testify in their apology, declare that they will no longer re-baptize, as was their former

custom; nevertheless, it is certain that many of them retain
their custom, and have united with the Anabaptists
(Hosius, Works of the Heresaeics of our Times, Bk. I. 431.
Ed. 1584). [*Op. Cit.*, pp. 85-86.]

Christian continues:

The claim of the Dutch Baptists to apostolic origin
was made the object of a special investigation in the year
1819, by Dr. Ypeij, Professor of Theology in Gronigen,
and the Rev. J.J. Dermout, Chaplain to the King of the
Netherlands, both of whom were learned members of the
Reformed Church. Many pages might be filled with the
reports that they made to the King. In the opinion of
these writers:
The Mennonites are descended from the tolerably
pure evangelical Waldenses, who were driven by persecution
into various countries; and who during the latter part of
the twelfth century fled into Flanders; and into the
provinces of Holland and Zealand, where they lived simple
and exemplary lives, in the villages as farmers, in the
towns by trades, free from the charge of any gross
immoralities, and professing the most pure and simple
principles, which they exemplified in holy conversation.
They were, therefore, in existence long before the
Reformed Church of the Netherlands.
We have now seen that the Baptists who were
formerly called Anabaptists, and in later times Mennonites,
were the original Waldenses, and who have long in the
history of the church received the honor of that origin. On
this account the Baptists may be considered as the only
Christian community which has stood since the days of the
apostles, and as a Christian society which has preserved
pure the doctrines of the Gospel through all ages. The
perfectly correct external and internal economy of the
Baptist denomination tends to confirm the truth, disputed
by the Romish Church, that the Reformation brought
about in the sixteenth century was in the highest degree
necessary, and at the same time goes to refute the
erroneous notion of the Catholics, that their denomination
is the most ancient (Ypeij en Dermout, Geschiedenis der
Nederlandsche Hervormde Kerk. Berda, 1819).
This testimony from the highest authority of the
Dutch Reformed Church, through a Commissioner
appointed by the King of the Netherlands, is a rare
instance of liberality and justice to another denomination.
It concedes all that Baptists have ever claimed in regard to
the continuity of their history. On this account State
patronage was tendered to the Baptists, which they

politely, but firmly declined. [*Op. Cit.*, pp. 95-96.]

We could give more testimonies by scholars of other denominations to the same effect but we believe that these should be sufficient.

Geographical Distribution of Baptists — During the first three centuries Baptists were primarily located around the Mediterranean Sea. In the period of obscurity we find them mainly in Southern Europe both in the east and the west and in the area of the Eastern Roman Empire that spills over into Asia. During the latter part of this period we find them also in Central and Northern Europe. In this last period though Baptists are found mainly in England and America from which countries most of the Baptist churches of modern times have come directly or indirectly. For this reason we will emphasize the story of Baptists in these two areas during this period. The freedom allowed in these two areas in this period seems to be largely the reason for the large and active group of Baptist churches.

BAPTISTS IN GREAT BRITAIN
1644 — 1689: FROM A CONFESSION OF SEVEN PARTICULAR BAPTIST CHURCHES TO THE TOLERATION ACT

Historical Background for 17th Century England — The political and religious background of this time is very important for a proper understanding of Baptist history. Charles I, the Stuart king, was very oppressive which eventually led to a Civil war. Parliament took the lead against the king in the war. The side of Parliament won and Charles I was eventually put to death. The king's opposition was fighting for more liberty both political and religious. The new government of England that finally emerges is controlled by a general for the Parliamentary cause, Oliver Cromwell. Soon after Cromwell's death the Stuart family is invited back to the throne of England. Charles II became king in 1660. We should also note that until Parliament obtained control the Episcopal church was the church of England. Parliament, though, established the Presbyterian church as the state church when they received the power. Because of the intolerance of the Presbyterian church to other religious groups, the army, which was made up largely of other denominations, objected strongly. Eventually this situation was altered by Cromwell in such a way that toleration as a whole was granted to other groups with the exception of Roman Catholics and those that didn't believe in the trinity. In 1660 the Episcopal church was again made the state church.

Baptists and Religious Liberty — The Baptists as a whole joined with the side of Parliament desiring to obtain religious liberty. Many fought in the civil war against the king and some held high positions in Cromwell's army. Baptists have always believed in religious liberty and at this time in England they did much to bring it about. Christian quotes Stoughton:

> The Baptists were foremost in the advocacy of religious freedom, and perhaps to one of them, Leonard Busher, citizen of London, belongs the honor of presenting, in this country, the first distinct and broad plea for liberty of conscience. [*Op. Cit.*, p. 221.]

In 1689 the Toleration Act brought religious toleration to England to a large extent. Catholics and Unitarians still did not have toleration. Baptists played an important role in bringing in toleration. Schaff says,

> For this change of public sentiment the chief merit is due to the English Non-conformists, who in the school of persecution became advocates of toleration, especially to the Baptists and Quakers, who made religious liberty (within the limits of the golden rule) an article of their creed, so that they could not consistently persecute even if they should have a chance to do so. [Philip Schaff, *Creeds of Christendom*, Vol. I, pp. 802-803.]

The Baptist belief is well-stated in the London confession of 1689.

> God alone is Lord of the conscience, and hath left it free from the Doctrines and Commandments of men which are in anything contrary to His word, or not contained in it. So that to believe such doctrines, or to obey such commands out of conscience is to betray true liberty of conscience; and requiring of an implicit faith, and absolute and blind obedience, is to destroy liberty of conscience and reason also.

Before the Toleration Act of 1689 the Baptists had to meet in secret much of the time. When they were discovered they were punished.

A Great Debate on Baptism — The Baptists ran into a major conflict with others during this period over the mode of baptism. Before this time the issue had usually centered around the subject of baptism. Immersion was usually admitted by all the scholars and church leaders to be the meaning of the word although they might practice otherwise for convenience. The Church of England practiced immersion usually until this century. When the Presbyterians came into power and the Episcopals were disestablished, sprinkling became the mode. Debates resulted as to the Scriptural meaning of baptism and the Baptists defended the truth. Schaff says, "In England immersion was the normal mode down to the middle of the seventeenth century." [Philip Schaff, *History of the Christian Church*, Vol. VII, p. 79.]

Christian says,

> There grew up in the reign of Charles I one of the most tremendous debates on baptism known in history. It raged continuously from about the year 1641 to the close of the century. The Presbyterians had brought in the innovation of pouring, and the Baptists, now for the first time permitted legally to speak, answered boldly. It has been sometimes said that the Baptists had just adopted immersion, but the evidence is to the contrary. There is no proof that in those days one English Baptist was in the practice of sprinkling. What really happened was that an occasion occurred, in the judgment of the Baptists, for a discussion of the act of Baptism, and the Baptists seized the opportunity. [J. T. Christian, *Op. Cit.*, pp. 297-298.]

The Particular and General Baptists — Baptists were divided into two groups during this time. One was called Particular Baptists and the other General Baptists. The names came from the beliefs of the two groups on the atonement. The Particular Baptists believed that the atonement was made only for the Lord's people and were Calvinistic with regard to the doctrine of salvation. The General Baptists believed that it was made for all people and were nominally Arminian in doctrine.

Associations of the Baptists — The General Baptists

were the larger of the two groups at this time. Several confessions of faith were made by them in this period. One made in 1660 was said to represent the beliefs of 20,000 and was made to show the new king that they were good citizens. The Particular Baptists were smaller but were very active. Eventually they were to become the stronger of the two groups and the group from which most of our Baptist churches of today would come. The Particular Baptists drew up confessions in 1644 and 1677. Representatives of 107 churches signed the confession of 1677. In 1689 the confession of 1677 was reaffirmed.

Several associations were formed by both Baptist groups in this century. They were primarily for fellowship, advice, and cooperating in various projects. A general assembly was formed in 1671 by the General Baptists and another in 1689 by the Particular Baptists.

Baptists were Persecuted — These were difficult times for the churches to hold services. An example of what they went through is seen in this quote which relates a little of the history of the Baptist church at Broadmead, Bristol.

This church was founded in 1640. The members met regularly for worship, whether they could obtain the services of a minister or not, the gifted brethren helping by prayer and exhortation. In 1651, Mr. Ewins, who had been a minister in the Episcopal Church, became their pastor. Under his ministry the church prospered. In addition to the Lord's Day exercise, they met on Thursday evenings in private houses for free conference on the Scriptures and mutual exhortation. These meetings were found very profitable.

But in 1661 their troubles began. On the 27th of July in that year, Mr. Ewins was apprehended while preaching. He was released on the 25th of September following, and immediately recommenced his work. Next year he endured another short imprisonment. A heavier trial came upon them in 1663. Mr. Ewins and several others were arrested on the 4th of October, and indicted at the quarter sessions for a riot. Various fines were imposed — Mr. Ewins was fined 50 pounds — and the parties adjudged to lie in prison till the fines were paid. So the prison became the parsonage till the following September, when a compromise was effected, and on payment of part of the money the prisoners were released. Mr. Ewins had not been idle, however. The people were accustomed to gather around the prison, and their pastor preached to them from the window of the room which he occupied, on the fourth story. "The word of the Lord was precious in those days."

Hitherto they had met in a "chapel called the Friars," but now they were compelled for a time to worship in private houses. The constables frequently disturbed them, and many were imprisoned and fined. Sometimes, when they learned that the officers were coming, they evaded them by taking refuge in a cellar, and sometimes by climbing into a garret. Still they resolutely kept up their assemblies. "In the year 1665," they say, "we had many disturbances, and divers imprisoned, but the Lord helped us through it." Their firmness was remarkable shown by a resolution passed to the effect that those who absented themselves from worship through fear should be dealt with as disorderly members. The names of all the members were engrossed on parchment, and the roll was called once a month, when they met for the Lord's supper, "to see who doth omit their duty." Not many were willing to expose themselves to church censure, but now and then a case occurred, and the delinquents were excluded "for neglecting their duty of assembling, through fear."

When the plague broke out in Bristol, in 1666, a stop was put to the persecution. There was peace for four years. In 1667 the church obtained another "public meeting place." It was "a large warehouse, up one pair of stairs." Mr. Ewins died April 26th, 1670. In the following month the police made their appearance again, and took some members of the congregation to the magistrates, who fined them. This was repeated several Lord's Days; but they secured the preacher by breaking a hole in the wall, so that he could stand in a room of the adjoining house, and preach without being seen. Thus their enemies were baffled. The opposition becoming more violent, they adopted another course. They nailed up the doors of the meeting house, and "we were fain," the record states, "to meet in the lanes and highways for several months." [J. M. Cramp, *Baptist History*, pp. 345-347.]

Discipline among the Baptists — The churches were strong on discipline. They believed that if a professed Christian did not live as a Christian should, he should be excluded until he repented. Cramp quotes a sentence that was passed from the records of a Baptist church.

That in the name of our Lord Jesus Christ, and by the authority he had given to the church, we did declare, that Sister Watkins, for her sin of disorderly walking, borrowing and not paying, making promises and not performing, and not diligently working, was withdrawn from, and no longer to have full communion with this church, nor to be partaker with them in the holy mysteries of the Lord's supper, nor privileges of the Lord's house (that is, 'if she doth come to the meeting, not be suffered to stay when any business of the church is transacted'); and the Lord have mercy upon her soul." [*Op. Cit.*, p. 382]

Baptists were excluded often for not attending services, marrying an unsaved person, lying, swearing, etc. Cramp says,

The church at Warboys withdrew from Mary Poulter, "for forsaking the assembling with the church and neglecting holy duties, and walking disorderly in pride and vanity;" and from John Christmas, "for not loving Ann his wife as he ought, and for speaking hateful and despising words against her, giving her occasion to depart from him by his unkindness." But "John Christmas, afterward sending for Ann his wife again and promising amendment, after her coming again to him, desired to be a partaker with the church, in holy duties, was joined in fellowship again." "Mary Drage, for sundry times dissembling with the church, and out of covetousness speaking things very untrue, at length it being plainly proved against her in her hearing, and she having little to say for herself, was withdrawn from." [*Op. Cit.*, 383-384.]

Minor Differences among Baptists — There were differences on some matters among Baptists that did not mar their fellowship. Congregational singing is an example. Some felt that this was wrong and would go outside the church until the singing was finished.

William Kiffen — Among the leaders of the Baptists we would like to note four of that time that were especially noteworthy. There were others but these were better known than most. William Kiffen was a great leader among the Baptists at this time. He was born in London in 1616 and lost both of his parents at the age of nine and almost his own life in a great plague. He was converted at an early age and became a Baptist in 1638. In 1640 the Devonshire Square Baptist Church was established and he became the pastor where he remained until his death in 1701. He was not only a pastor but also a merchant. He became very wealthy and well-known as a merchant in

London. He was also well known by the kings of the time.

He suffered much for his beliefs. He was stoned, arrested, fined, and imprisoned. In his days those that informed the authorities about Baptist meetings got part of the fine. This encouraged many to make this a business. Some of these informers were able to make a considerable amount of money. Cramp says of them,

> They spent their time in prowling about the retired streets and by-lanes of towns, or in exploring the recesses of woods, and wild, desolate places, if happily they might hear the voice of singing or prayer, or watch the movements of some straggler, hastening to join his brethren. With savage glee they darted upon the secret assembly, gloating over their confusion and distress, and specially rejoicing when they seized the preacher, because of the heavier fine. [Op. Cit., p. 342.]

The informers were constantly after Kiffen and his church. Once when he was brought to court by them he was able to escape the fine when errors were discovered in the proceedings. Cook says

> This result discouraged the informers from proceeding against other brethren. But his enemies were determined to entrap him. They attended his meetings and secretly kept a record of them, and finally prosecuted him for them all at once, attempting to have him fined $1,500.00. But he again defeated them at law through errors in the records, and they were compelled to abandon the suit. [R. B. Cook, The Story of the Baptists in all Ages and Countries, p. 140.]

He was an able and brave defender of Baptist principles and used the wealth God had given him to forward the Lord's work.

Hanserd Knolleys — Hanserd Knolleys was also an able leader among the Baptists. He was educated at the University of Cambridge for the Episcopal Church. After several years as a minister in that church he became convinced by studying the Scriptures that his church was in error. He left the Church of England and eventually became a Baptist. He suffered much and was forced to flee England several times for safety. On one flight he came to New England but not finding freedom there he returned to

England in 1641.

He was a very learned man who wrote several books. He prepared grammars for Greek, Hebrew, and Latin. He established a Baptist church in London and was their pastor from 1645 — 1691 when he died. He also established a school. Armitage says concerning him,

> But one day, preaching in Bow Church, Cheapside, he spoke against infant baptism, which gave such offense that he was thrown into prison. On his release he went into Suffolk, where he was mobbed as an "Anabaptist," and after being stoned was sent to London on a warrant to answer to Parliament. Last of all he established a Baptist Church, meeting in Great St. Helen's, London, where he seldom preached to less than a thousand people. There, says Wilson, he gave great offense to his Presbyterian brethren, "and the landlord was prevailed upon to warn him out of the place" . . . Again and again he was forbidden to preach, and as often he disregarded the charge and was pursued or imprisoned. At times he fled to Wales, Holland and Germany, to escape his foes. But his life was spared to the ripe age of ninety-three, and he preached the word in all parts of the kingdom; on Sundays generally delivering three or four sermons, and as many during the week, for a period of forty years. When in prison he had to content himself with one a day. Because of his great meekness and learning he won many distinguished persons to Baptist views. [Thomas Armitage, *Op. Cit.*, p. 470.]

Benjamin Keach — Benjamin Keach was a pastor of a Baptist church in London that later was to be pastored by John Gill and C. H. Spurgeon. Benjamen Keach wrote forty-three works some of which were large. One of his works was called, "The Child's Instructor; or a New and Easy Primer." Since the book expounded Baptist doctrine he was brought to court and sentenced. He was jailed, fined, pilloried, and his book was burned before him in public. The pillory was a cruel and dangerous punishment. Usually the crowds threw rotten eggs and stones at the victim which sometimes resulted in death. The crowd, knowing the high type of man that he was, treated him with respect. Keach used the opportunity to preach to the people. He continued to speak to the crowds at intervals dispite the threats of the officials. He told the crowd, "I do account this the greatest honor that ever the Lord was pleased to confer upon me." He suffered much, being imprisoned many times.

> Once he was seized by four dragoons, who bound
> him and laid him on the ground, intending to trample him
> to death with their horses. But just as they were about to
> put spurs to their horses to execute their murderous design
> a humane officer rode up and ordered them to desist.
> [R. B. Cook *Op. Cit.*, p. 145.]
> One striking fact is related of his later years. He was
> so ill in 1689 that life was despaired of, even by his
> physicians. Mr. Knollys, who greatly loved him, knelt at
> his bedside, and after fervently praying that God would
> add to his life the time granted to Hezekiah; on rising,
> said, "Brother Keach, I shall be in heaven before you."
> Both the prayer and prediction were honored to the letter;
> Knollys died two years afterward and Keach lived fifteen
> years. [Thomas Armitage, *Op. Cit.*, pp. 550-551.]

John Bunyan — The Baptist of this period best known
today is John Bunyan. His work Pilgrim's Progress has made
him famous. However, in justice we must say he was not
the leader among Baptists that the others mentioned were.
Neither did he influence the Baptists of subsequent years
like his brethren. He believed in open communion and this
was contrary to the beliefs of most of the Baptists of his
day. In 1653 he was saved and soon after this he was
permitted to preach. In 1660 he was arrested and put in
Bedford jail where he remained for twelve years. The
charges that sent him to jail were abstaining from coming to
the church of England, upholding meetings contrary to law,
and teaching others to worship contrary to law. In other
words he was a Baptist that practiced his convictions.

> His courageous wife pleaded in vain with his judges
> for his release. While in prison, he worked industriously
> making laces to support himself and his family. His little
> blind daughter, Mary, comforted him by her presence. He
> was not allowed to have any books in the jail, except a
> Bible and Fox's "Book of Martyrs." With no helps to
> study but these, he wrote the "Pilgrim's Progress," besides
> other works. Release from prison could have been procured
> for him at any time by promising not to preach, but he
> refused to accept liberty at any such a price. He believed
> that God had given him the right to preach the gospel,
> and rather than surrender that right to any man, he was
> willing to endure imprisonment and even death. In the last

year of his confinement, and while still in jail, he was chosen pastor by the church at Bedford. He was released in 1672. [R. B. Cook, *Op. Cit.*, pp. 168-169.]

He died in 1688 just a few months before the English Revolution and the coming of freedom.

1689 — 1792: FROM THE TOLERATION ACT TO THE BEGINNING OF THE MODERN FOREIGN MISSION MOVEMENT

Religious Decline in the 18th Century — After toleration came, a religious decline began throughout England. Perhaps it was partly due to the fact that Christians weren't used to the new freedom and the Christian life became much easier in a way. There were philosophies of the time that found root in some churches. Deism and Socinianism were accepted by many and unbelief and worldliness resulted. The Anglicans, Presbyterians, and General Baptists suffered great damage. The General Baptists declined because a number of their ministers in the last period and in this period became convinced of the doctrines of grace as taught by the Particular Baptists and joined them. These evil philosphies also did much to weaken their ranks. A majority of General Baptists became Unitarians. They faded from the scene as far as doing anything of significance. The Particular Baptists grew some and practically were unaffected by the evil philosophies of the day. They did as well or better than any denomination of the time in this regard. There was a lack of evangelistic and missionary zeal among the Particular Baptists though. This was corrected in the latter part of the period with the beginning of the missionary movement.

John Gill — The soundness in doctrine among the Particular Baptists we believe was due largely to the work of John Gill. He was called in 1719 to pastor the church Keach had pastored years before. He continued in this church until his death in 1771. He was a scholar in Greek, Hebrew, and Latin. He had studied the Talmuds, Targums, and other Jewish works as few have ever studied them. His knowledge in other subjects was vast and deep. Toplady said of him, "If any man can be supposed to have trod the whole circle of human learning, it was Dr. Gill."

He produced a complete commentary of the Bible and a large work on doctrine plus other works. His "Expositions of the Old and New Testaments" and "Body of Divinity" are still in print. His commentary covers every verse in the Bible in an exhaustive fashion. It is widely used by Baptist ministers today. He was willing to stand for the truth no matter what the cost. When he entered into one controversy he was warned:

> that he would lose the esteem and subscriptions of some wealthy persons if he did not desist. Dr. Gill replied; 'Don't tell me of losing; I value nothing in comparison with gospel truths. I am not afraid to be poor." [*Op. Cit.*, p. 193.]

Wesleyan Revivals — During the middle part of the eighteenth century John Wesley and George Whitefield began preaching. The religious life of the nation was greatly affected by these preachers and others that joined them. Even though the Particular Baptists did not accept Wesley because of his Arminianism and the General Baptists because of their general deadness and unorthodoxy, Baptists were affected to some extent by him and his movement.

Dan Taylor — Dan Taylor was a convert of the Wesleyan revival who could not accept some of the views of the Methodists. For this reason he and others withdrew from them and after studying the Scriptures became convinced that Baptist views were Biblical. He joined the General Baptist church at Gamston by baptism in 1763. After this he baptized the others that he had been associated with and organized them into a Baptist church. He desired fellowship with the General Baptists until he learned of their unorthodox beliefs. Many of them did not believe in the atonement of Christ, that justification was by faith only, and that the Holy Spirit regenerated the saint at his conversion. Taylor and others of like persuasion started "The Assembly of the Free Grace General Baptists" in 1770. These churches were also called the "New Connection." This group began with eight churches under the leadership of Dan Taylor. John Clifford at the end of the next century led them to unite with the Particular Baptists.

The Baptist Missionary Movement — The most

momentous event during the last part of this century was the beginning of the modern Baptist missionary movement. Richard Cook traces the beginning thus:

> The first step was taken in the year 1779 by Rev. Robert Hall, father of the celebrated preacher of that name. A sermon which he preached before the Northamptonshire Association, did much to give shape to the growing tendency of the denomination. His text was Isaiah 57:14; "Cast ye up, prepare ye the way, take up the stumbling block out of the way of my people." The sermon was enlarged and published and widely circulated. From that time we may discern religious progress. Thoughtful concern for the souls of others began to manifest itself.
>
> But there was another cause which probably contributed to the development of the spirit of missions.
>
> In the year 1784, at a meeting of the Northamptonshire Association, the monthly concert of prayer for missions was inaugurated. This, doubtless, has been one of the most efficient causes in the development and growth of the missionary cause. . .
>
> Rev. Andrew Fuller, about this time, published a tract which helped the missionary movement. It was entitled "The Gospel of Christ, Worthy of all acceptation; or, The Obligations of men fully to credit and cordially to approve whatever God makes known: wherein is considered the nature of Faith in Christ and true Duty of those where gospel comes in this matter."
>
> To William Carey, however, more than to any one, is due the origin of modern missions. He was the first to catch the inspiration, and his zeal and enthusiasm surpassed all others. In 1791, a friend who knew of his interest in missions, placed fifty dollars in his hands, saying, "Write about it." This enabled him to publish his "Inquiry into the obligations of Christians to use means for the conversion of the heathen;" a treatise which had great influence. The missionary spirit began to rise among ministers and people, and the very next year, 1792, at the anniversary of the association at Nottingham, in May, Carey preached before them a sermon of overwhelming power, from Isaiah 54:33; on the obligation of the church to "Expect Great Things From God, and Attempt Great Things for God." His earnest words produced a profound impression. "Is it not practicable and obligatory" he asked, "to attempt the conversion of the heathen?" And when it seemed that they were going to separate without reaching any definite result, Mr. Carey, in an agony of distress and indignation, seizing Mr. Fuller by the hand, demanded if

they were going to part without doing anything in the matter. This appeal was irresistible, and the result was that a resolution was adopted to appoint a committee to prepare a plan for a Baptist missionary society. It was but little thought of at the time, but to us it is an event of vast importance, as we view it in connection with the results that have flowed from it. [*Op. Cit.*, pp. 302-305.]

On October 12, 1792 the committee met in Kettering and formed "The Particular Baptist Society for the Propagation of the Gospel among the Heathen." They took up a small collection. William Carey and Dr. John Thomas, a physician, were sent out to India as the first missionaries on June 13, 1793. Dr. Thomas had been in India where he preached the gospel to the heathen as he was able. Since he was concerned for the natives he returned to England to urge the Baptists to send out missionaries.

William Carey was prepared by God for this task in a marvelous way. He was born in an Episcopalian home on August 17, 1761. At the age of twenty-two he was saved and baptized in a Baptist Church. He was a shoemaker with a great thirst for knowledge. As he would work on his shoes he would study his books. His ability in languages was outstanding. He was able to learn Hebrew, Greek, Latin, German, French, and other languages by himself. He became a school teacher next. He made a leather globe to teach geography and as he considered this subject the thought struck him that 400 million had never heard of Christ. This seems to be the beginning of his interest in foreign missions. For awhile he preached, taught school, worked as a cobbler, and carried on a hard course of study all at the same time. This is the way God prepared him for his work.

Carey met with many trials after he was appointed to go to India. He couldn't get the permission of the East India Co. so he had to go without it. His wife at first refused to go, so he planned to go without her. At the last minute she decided to go reluctantly. After arriving in India, Cook says,

Mr. Thomas proposed to support himself by practicing medicine, while Mr. Carey went to work at clearing the jungles, at the same time, keeping out of the way of the company for fear of arrest. In 1794, Mr. Carey took charge of an indigo factory, and Mr. Thomas took charge of another, and through their employer, they obtained permission to remain in the country. Marshman, his co-laborer in missions, gives a sad picture of the distressing circumstances to which Mr. Carey was for a time subjected: "He was in a foreign land, without a friend and without a farthing, except as he could wring it from Mr. Thomas, and it required all the strength derived from a firm confidence in the Divine promises, to keep him from being overwhelmed with despondency. His wife, who had accompanied him to India with great reluctance, was constantly upbraiding him with their wretchedness, and contrasting their indigence with the comparative luxury in which Mr. Thomas was living. His family, consisting of seven persons, was crowded into a small, ill ventilated house, without any of the conveniences requisite for the European constitution in an Eastern climate, and his wife and two of his children were attacked with dysentery, from which they recovered but slowly. [*Op. Cit.*, p. 313.]

It was seven years before they had their first convert but after that the work advanced rapidly and there were many converts. Vedder speaks of his accomplishments when he says,

He wisely spent his time and strength in translating the Scriptures and other Christian literature into the Indian languages and dialects, in making grammars, and the like. Thus he not only did a great work for his own generation, but one that will last for all time, or so long as these languages shall be spoken. Before his death, there had been issued under his supervision, he himself doing a large part of the work, versions of the Scriptures in forty different languages or dialects, spoken by a third of the people on the globe; and of these Scriptures two hundred and twelve thousand copies had been issued. [H. C. Vedder, *Op. Cit.*, p. 254.]

Andrew Fuller — Although Andrew Fuller did not go to the mission field he was very prominent in the mission work. He was the first financial secretary of the work and he continued in that capacity until his death. He had agreed to hold the rope while Carey went down into the well. He worked very hard to hold the rope by traveling, writing, preaching, and collecting in behalf of the mission work. Upon one occasion he told a nobleman of the mission work who gave a guinea as a gift:

Observing that it was given with an air of

indifference, Mr. Fuller asked; "My Lord, does this come
from the heart?" "What matter is that?" replied the
nobleman; "suppose it does not come from the heart, it
may answer your purpose as well. If you get the money,
why should you care whether it comes from the heart or
not?" "Take it back," said the man of God. "I cannot
take it. My Lord and Master requires the heart." "Well,
give it back to me," said the nobleman, "it did not come
from the heart." He took the guinea, and stepping to his
desk, drew a check on his banker for twenty pounds,
about one hundred dollars, and handing it to Mr. Fuller,
said; "This comes from the heart. I know the principles by
which you are governed. I love the Lord Jesus Christ and
his cause, and know that no offering is acceptable to him
unless it comes from the heart." [R. B. Cook, *Op. Cit.*, pp.
307-308.]

Fuller was very important in helping to correct an
idea that had developed among some Baptists that missions
were contrary to the Divine purposes. Andrew Fuller wrote
to show that preaching to the heathen was commanded and
in harmony with the doctrines of election, particular
redemption, etc. His theology has greatly influenced Baptists
until this day. He believed that the atonement was only
designed for the Elect but that its value was infinite. He
believed strongly in the doctrines of unconditional election
and also in missions since both were taught in God's Word.

English Baptist Hymns — Many of the hymns were
written by English Baptists. Some of the more popular
today are "Blest be the tie that binds" by John Fawcett,
"How firm a foundation, ye saints of the Lord" by George
Keith, "My hope is built on nothing less" by Edward Mote,
"Come, thou fount of every blessing" by Robert Robinson,
and "On Jordan's stormy banks I stand" by Samuel
Stennett.

1792 — 1891: FROM THE BEGINNING OF THE MODERN FOREIGN MISSION MOVEMENT TO THE UNITING OF MOST OF THE BAPTISTS IN ENGLAND IN THE BAPTIST UNION

Baptist Growth — During the last period the growth
had been very slow but with the beginning of the foreign
missionary society we have the beginning of great growth
among the Baptists. This comparison will help to show this
growth. From 1689 to 1800 there were 233 new churches

established that continued until 1900. From 1800 to 1900 there were 1661 new churches established that continued until 1900. Of the 233 more than 100 were established between 1780 to 1800. We believe that this great growth is largely due to the emphasis upon foreign missions.

Home Missions — When the churches began to emphasize foreign missions the work at home greatly increased. Itinerant preaching tours by Baptist pastors and societies to support and encourage such preaching were the means used to advance home missions.

> The initial type of home mission work took the form of itinerant preaching tours conducted by individual ministers in the northern counties. For example, William Steadman, who later became the first president of the Northern Education Society (now Rawdon College), and his students at Bristol Academy engaged in several such tours. Out of the inspiration of such itinerancy, the Particular Baptists developed a second method which was embodied in the creation in London in 1797 of the Society for the Encouragement and Support of Itinerant Preaching, a name which was later changed to the Home Mission Society. By 1835 it was employing one hundred full-time missionaries. [R. G. Torbet, *A History of the Baptists*, p. 109.]

Baptist Schools — Several schools were started during this period which greatly aided the growth by training ministers. These schools are Midland College 1797, Rawdon College 1804, Regent's Park College 1810, Spurgeon's College 1856, Bangor College 1862, Manchester's Strict Communionest College 1866, and Cardiff 1897. Bristol College is the oldest school having been started as an academy in 1680.

Foreign Mission Expansion — While the Baptist work flourished at home the foreign work that began with Carey and Thomas also grew. Many missionaries were sent out to India and the new fields of Ceylon, West Indies, Africa, China, Japan, Palestine, and Europe.

Bible Society — In 1804 the British and Foreign Bible Society was begun. It was composed of Christians from about ten different denominations who desired to send out the Bible to all countries without any comments on the text. The first secretary of the Society was Joseph Hughes, a Baptist pastor, who had been very prominent in the beginning of the society. Because in 1835 there was disagreement among the members of the society over translating the word baptize, immerse, the Baptists of England began a new society in 1840, the Bible Translation Society.

Sunday School Movement — Baptists were active also in the Sunday school movement and in tract societies. A plan for a Sunday school society was presented by a Baptist deacon. William Fox. Before his plan was adopted he heard of Raikes Sunday Schools, which plan was proposed and adopted in 1785.

Charles Haddon Spurgeon — During this period there were several well-known and able pastors in England, Wales, Scotland, and Ireland that should be mentioned. Charles Haddon Spurgeon was born in 1834. His father and grandfather had been Congregationalist preachers. Spurgeon was saved when he was seventeen and united with the Baptists. When he became a Baptist because of his study of the Bible his mother was very grieved. She told her son that she had prayed for his conversion but not that he might be a Baptist. Spurgeon answered his mother, "Well, dear mother, you know that the Lord is so good, that he always gives us more than we can ask or think." At nineteen he was the pastor of the London Baptist Church that had been formerly pastored by Benjamen Keach, John Gill, and John Rippon. Here he continued until his death in 1892.

The Lord used him in a mighty way as a preacher, teacher, writer, and leader in the beginning of many useful works. Under his leadership his church grew to over five thousand members. Every week his sermons were published for many years reaching more than a half a million people. His sermons are still being printed and are in great demand. In theology he was a strong Calvinist as to the way of salvation and a great student of the Puritans. He was very evangelistic and his ministry was blessed by many conversions. He wrote a number of books that are still in print, such as his seven volume commentary on the Psalms, The Treasury of David. He published a paper and began an organization to distribute Bibles, good books, and tracts. A Pastor's college which trained many ministers was another achievement. He also began an orphanage which took care of hundreds of children. His life and work are still an inspiration and help to countless people. When he died the institutions that he began continued on with little change.

Alexander Maclaren — Alexander Maclaren lived at the same time as Spurgeon. He was the pastor of a Baptist church in Manchester and was noted as one of the great expository preachers. He wrote some; perhaps his best known work is his commentary on the Psalms which is considered one of the best ever written. Many of his sermons are in print.

Robert Hall, John Clifford — Robert Hall and John Clifford were also leading preachers of this period. Hall was known as one of the greatest of pulpit orators. Clifford was a leader who held several prominent positions in behalf of the Baptists of his day.

Sir Henry Havelock — There have been consecrated Baptist laymen all through our history that have been very useful in the Lord's work. We can't give the space that we would like to these godly men but we would like to mention one as an example. Sir Henry Havelock who lived during this period made the army his career and rose to Major General. He became famous for his victories in India during the Sepoy Rebellion.

> His custom was to spend two hours alone with God every morning, whether in camp or campaign, and, as often as he could find time, to read and expound the Scriptures to his men. His biographer gives a touching account of an officer hearing hymns floating around a heathen pagoda, and on entering, finding Havelock, with about a hundred soldiers, reading the Scriptures to them by the light of the dim lamps burning before the idols. No wonder that the troops of this splendid Christian soldier were renowned for their prudence and bravery, even to daring, or that their invincibility was ascribed to the fact that they were 'Havelock's Saints.' [Thomas Armitage, *Op. Cit.*, p. 591.]

Robert and James Haldane — In Scotland the Haldane brothers were greatly used of God. Robert traveled to the continent to make the Word of God known. In Switzerland he lectured on Romans to a group of ministerial students. These lectures changed the lives of several of the students who later became prominent in the work of the Lord. Robert, who was wealthy, used his money to educate three hundred and forty-nine ministers. He also gave to other worthy causes. He wrote a commentary on Romans that is considered one of the best. James was instrumental in beginning thirty-eight churches; he also wrote.

Christmas Evans — Wales had over 100,000 Baptists by 1900. One of the best known Baptist preachers of Wales during this time was Christmas Evans. He was a Baptist preacher with practically no formal training. He taught himself and in spite of many obstacles became a great and useful preacher. When his father died he was fifteen and could not read. With great determination he learned, and after his conversion he began to preach sermons of other men that he memorized. Another obstacle came into his life when he lost an eye at the hands of a mob in his early life. Most of the time he served several churches for very little money. In spite of these things in time he became a remarkable student and preacher of the Word. In later life he was able to preach his famous sermon on the demoniac of Gadara to a vast audience and keep them spell-bound for three hours. His ministry was blessed with many conversions.

Alexander Carson — Alexander Carson was a very well-educated preacher. He graduated from the University of Glasgow as first in his class. After finishing school he accepted the pastorate of a Presbyterian church at Tubbermore, Ireland, at very good pay. From his study of the Scriptures he became convinced of Baptist distinctives and left his position and became a Baptist. In doing this he passed up a very good position and a very promising future. He organized a small church which grew to five hundred members. He is one of the greatest scholars that Baptists have ever had. He wrote much but his most famous work is on the doctrine of baptism, a work which has never been surpassed in its field.

The Baptist Union — This period ends with the New Connection General Baptists joining the Particular Baptists in the Baptist Union in 1891. During this period a number of societies had been formed for the purpose of Baptist churches cooperating in foreign missions, home missions, education, etc. Through various mergers these societies came into one organization, the Baptist Union. In 1813 when the Baptist Union began it was only one society that promoted home missions. By 1891 only a few churches in England remained outside of the Baptist Union. Its purpose had expanded from home missions, to foreign missions, and all the other worthy objects for which Baptist churches cooperate. The union was voluntary and churches could withdraw whenever they liked. The churches were recognized as self-governing by the union.

1891 – 1960: FROM THE UNITING OF MOST OF THE BAPTISTS IN ENGLAND IN THE BAPTIST UNION TO THE PRESENT

Numbers emphasized rather than Doctrine – The great growth of the last period caused Baptists to cooperate in various societies for the sake of even greater growth. For the sake of efficiency and more growth most of the churches were finally working together in one society, the Baptist Union. Since some churches and individuals differed greatly it brought about a problem. To continue in cooperation with some who held to unorthodox views would have a bad effect on the orthodox churches and on their united accomplishments. The basis of cooperation in the Union was not doctrinal but more efficiency in growth.

Spurgeon Withdraws from the Baptist Union – Spurgeon recognized this and withdrew from the Baptist Union in 1887. He wrote in his paper, "The Sword and Trowel," for November 1887:

> As a matter of fact, believers in Christ's atonement are now in declared religious union with those who make light of it; believers in Holy Scriptures are in confederacy with those who deny plenary inspiration; those who hold evangelical doctrine are in open alliance with those who call the fall a fable, who deny the personality of the Holy Ghost, who call justification by faith immoral and hold that there is another probation after death, and a future restitution for the lost . . . To be very plain, we are unable to call these things Christian Unions, they begin to look like Confederacies in Evil. Before the face of God we fear that they wear no other aspect. To our inmost heart this is a sad truth from which we cannot break away . . . We retire at once and distinctly from the Baptist Union.

Open Communion – There had been some churches in the seventeenth century and up until today that have practiced open communion and mixed membership. Mixed membership churches are not New Testament Baptist churches. In the past these churches have been in a minority and have been strongly condemned by the orthodox Baptists. Starting in the last period open communion churches have increased and also what often follows, mixed membership churches. While some churches calling themselves Baptist have taken a liberal theology and some are made up of baptized believers and unbaptized believers, others still continue to adhere to Baptist distinctives.

Union with Other Denominations Refused — In this last period there have been several invitations offered the Baptists to unite with other denominations. The Baptists of England have refused every such offer, believing such a union would be contrary to their beliefs.

World War II — This period has also seen two World Wars. The Baptists had chaplains in both. In the World War II the bombings of England greatly affected the Baptists and others. 740 Baptist churches were destroyed or damaged. Sunday schools were stopped in many cases in the big cities as the children were evacuated to the country for safety. Blackouts hindered the evening services.

A great reconstruction campaign was begun to rebuild and repair churches damaged in the war. The Baptists have responded well. Missions have also been continued very well. Even during the war years the Baptists carred on giving sacrificially in spite of the difficulties.

BAPTISTS IN AMERICA
1638 — 1740:FROM THE BEGINNING OF THE BAPTIST CHURCH AT NEWPORT, R. I. TO THE GREAT AWAKENING

John Clarke — It seems to us that the information available indicates that the first Baptist church in America was started in 1638 at Newport, Rhode Island. There were people in the colonies before this who were Baptists but not churches to our knowledge. Dr. John Clarke was the first pastor of this church. He was a physician who came from England for religious freedom. Not finding freedom in Massachusetts he led a group to Rhode Island. This group settled in Newport and Portsmouth in 1638. A church was started in Newport that same year. Clarke was pastor until his death. The colonists sent him to England in 1651 for a better charter for Rhode Island. He couldn't receive it from Cromwell but he did from Charles II twelve years later in 1663. This charter granted political and religious freedom to Rhode Island. He was a leader among the Baptists and in the government of Rhode Island.

Roger Williams — Quite often Roger Williams and the First Baptist Church in Providence, Rhode Island, are given the honor of being the first Baptist church and pastor in America. Williams was an Englishman who was educated at Cambridge. He came to America to find religious freedom but he found none. He was banished from Massachusetts for teaching that the magistrate hasn't any authority to punish those who break the commandments dealing with a man's relationship to God. He settled in what is now Providence, Rhode Island, and entered into a compact with others that granted religious liberty to all in 1638.

He became convinced that baptism was the immersion of a believer. Ezekiel Holliman baptized Williams and Williams baptized the others and they formed a church in 1639. A few months after this Williams withdrew from the church believing that he was not Scripturally baptized since Holliman wasn't baptized when he baptized Williams. He never joined any other church but considered himself a seeker the rest of his days.

This church continued for several years and then it seems to have passed out of existence. The First Baptist Church of Providence claims to be William's church, however it cannot be proved. The oldest church records begin in 1775 for this church. None of the other early churches, however, came from the one Williams started.

The Origin of other Baptist Churches in New England — There were several churches that were started in our country with people who had become Baptists in England or Wales. The church at Swansea in the Massachusetts colony is an example. Pastor John Myles and several members of his Baptist church in Wales came to this country because of persecution. They organized a Baptist church in Rehoboth in 1663 and then moved to Swansea.

The first Baptist church in Boston was started in 1665 with Thomas Goold as pastor. This area was very intolerant at this time so the Baptists suffered much. The pastor and members were fined and imprisoned many times because of their beliefs.

During this early time the Baptists suffered for their convictions. Cook tells of the persecution of Obadiah Holmes, the man who was to be the pastor of the Newport Baptist church after John Clarke:

> *Obadiah Holmes Suffers* — The colony of Massachusetts continued to persecute the Baptists with greater severity, and large numbers suffered from fines, imprisonment, whipping or banishment. One of the most remarkable cases was that of Obadiah Holmes, who went with two other Baptists from Rhode Island to visit, in 1651, an aged brother at Lynn, who had been whipped for being a Baptist. While holding religious services at this brother's house on the Sabbath, they were arrested and fined and imprisoned. The others were in a short time released, but Mr. Holmes was retained to be severely punished as a public example. He was sentenced to be whipped in Boston in September 1651, and so barbarously was the sentence executed that for days and weeks he "could take no rest but as he lay upon his knees and elbows, not being able to suffer any part of his body to touch the bed whereon he lay." The sentence pronounced upon him, contains these words; — "You did take upon you to preach and baptize; that you did baptize such as were baptized before, and thereby did necessarily deny the baptism before administered to be baptism; and did also deny the lawfulness of baptizing infants."
>
> As he was led to the place of punishment he said to the crowds of people who were assembled to witness the scene; "That which I am to suffer for, is the word of God and the testimony of Jesus Christ." In his own account of the affair, he says; "As the man began to lay the strokes upon my back, I said to the people, 'Though my flesh should fail, and my spirit should fail, yet God would not fail.' So it pleased the Lord to come in and to fill my heart and tongue as a vessel full, and with audible voice I spoke forth, praying the Lord not to lay this sin to their charge; and telling the people that now I found He did not fail me and therefore, now I should trust Him forever who failed me not. For in truth, as the strokes fell upon me, I had such a spiritual manifestation of God's presence, as I never had before, and the outward pain was so removed from me that I could well bear it, yea, and in a manner, felt it not, although it was grievous, as the spectators said, the man striking with all his strength, spitting upon his hand three times, with a three-corded

whip, giving me there with thirty strokes. When he had loosed me from the post, having joyousness in my countenance as the spectators observed, I told the magistrates; you have struck me with roses, and said, moreover, although the Lord hath made it easy to me, yet I pray God it may not be laid to your charge." Many were touched with sympathy for the noble sufferer, and the Baptist cause was greatly strengthened by the very means that were used to crush it. As Mr. Holmes says; "My bonds and imprisonment have been no hindrance to the gospel; for before my return some submitted to the Lord and were baptized, and divers were put upon the way of inquiry." [R. B. Cook, *Op. Cit.*, pp. 206-208.]

Persecution for Baptists ended in Massachusetts in 1691 when Massachusetts Bay Colony and Plymouth Colony were united under a new charter which gave all but Roman Catholics religious liberty. Baptists still had to pay taxes though to support the state church for some time.

Baptists in Philadelphia — In the middle colonies several Baptist churches began in this period. There were churches in New York, Pennsylvania, and New Jersey but the most important and most influential area for the Baptists was around Philadelphia. A very important church was the Lower Dublin or Pennepeck church of Philadelphia. It was organized in 1688 with twelve members and Elias Keach as Pastor. He was the son of Benjamin Keach of London. Their first building was made of logs. Elias Keach their pastor came to the people in a most unusual way.

He arrived in this country, a wild youth, about the year 1686. On his landing he dressed in black and wore bands, in order to pass as a minister. The project succeeded to his wishes and many people resorted to hear the young London divine. He performed well enough till he had advanced pretty far in the sermon; then stopping short, he looked like a man astonished. The audience concluded that he had been seized with a sudden disorder; but, on asking what the matter was, received from him a confession of the imposture, with tears in his eyes, and much trembling. Great was his distress, though it ended happily: for from that time he dated his conversion. [*Op. Cit.*, pp. 255-256.]

After this experience he went for counsel to the Pastor of the Baptist church at Cold Spring, Pennsylvania.

Thomas Duggan was the pastor who had come from the
Baptists of Newport, R. I. and organized Cold Spring church
in 1684. Elias Keach was baptized and ordained. He
organized the Lower Dublin church and became a leader
among the Baptists in that area until he returned to
England.

The churches of the area began soon to have "general
meetings" annually and then semi-annually for fellowship
and preaching.

The Philadelphia Association —
These were for many years what their name implied
— general meetings — being attended by as many as could
make it convenient and were wholly devotional and
evangelistic. In 1707 the meeting was for the first time a
delegated body, five churches appointing delegates and this
is the beginning of the Philadelphia Association. From the
first the New Jersey churches were members and as the
body increased in age and strength it attracted to itself all
the Baptist churches within traveling distance of it, having
as members churches in southern New York and Virginia.
Its adoption of a strongly Calvinistic confession in 1742
(or possibly earlier) was a turning-point in the history of
American Baptists, as it ensured the prevalence of that
type of theology. Up to this time Arminian Baptists had
been the stronger in New England and the colonies of New
York and New Jersey, and it was at one time probable
that they would control the development of the
denomination. It was the Philadelphia Association that
turned the tide and decided the course of American
Baptist history. The Association speedily became the
leading body among American Baptists — a position it has
not wholly lost to this day. Pretty much everything good
in our history, from 1700 to 1850, may be traced to its
initiative or active cooperation. [H. C. Vedder, *Op. Cit.*,
pp. 305-306.]

The Philadelphia Confession of faith has been adopted
by many Baptists since then as an expression of their
beliefs. This confession was the Second London Confession
of Particular Baptists of 1689. This association was the first
Baptist association in America. By 1757 it was composed of
twenty-five churches scattered throughout Pennsylvania, New
Jersey, Connecticut, New York, Virginia, and Maryland.

The significance of the Association cannot be
over-emphasized, for without violating Baptist church

autonomy it provided a source of guidance and unity at a critical period of organization in the denomination. In addition, it afforded a pattern of democratic polity which was destined to be well received in the liberty-loving colonies. [R. G. Torbet, *Op. Cit.*, p. 232.

The First Baptist Church in the South — The first Baptist church of the south was started in 1684 at Charleston, South Carolina. This church had moved from Kittery, Maine because of persecution. It was organized there in 1682 and then reorganized in 1684 when it moved to South Carolina. In Virginia we know of no Baptist church until 1714. There is evidence of Baptists before this in the colony but not of a church. In 1714 a Baptist Church was organized at Burleigh. It is called the Mill Swamp Church today. By the end of the period there were several churches scattered throughout Virginia, North Carolina, and South Carolina.

Summary — During this period about sixty Baptist churches began in the American colonies with a membership of about 5,000. They were persecuted to some degree in several of the colonies. In Massachusetts and Virginia they found very harsh treatment. The Congregationalist church was the state church of the former and the Episcopal of the latter. The union of church and state has often led to persecution of those that differ with the ones in power. The persecution of the Baptists for their convictions at this time consisted of imprisonment, banishment, whippings, fines, and forced taxation to support the state church. This situation was eased considerably with the rise of William and Mary to power in England in 1689. The population of the colonies was very small and the land occupied was just the narrow strip along the Atlantic seaboard from New England to Georgia. Inland was very wild country inhabited by Indians. In the next period of this history the Baptists move into that territory as our country expands westward.

1740 — 1845: FROM THE GREAT AWAKENING TO THE DIVISION AMONG BAPTISTS OVER SLAVERY

The Great Awakening — There was a great revival in the 1730's called the Great Awakening. Two of the most prominent preachers in the Great Awakening were Jonathan

Edwards and George Whitefield. There were other preachers also that were greatly used. There were many converts and Christians were revived. It did not begin with the Baptists but they greatly benefited by it. Many of these converts upon studying the Scriptures became Baptists and the Baptist ranks grew mightily. Whitefield's methods of evangelism divided the Baptists into two groups. Those who accepted his methods were called "New Lights" or "separates" while the others were called "Regulars."

The Philadelphia Association and Home Missions — The Philadelphia Association played a very important part in the growth of the Baptists. The churches of this Association sent out many missionaries who began a number of Baptist churches. They also were active in beginning two schools that trained many pastors and leaders among them.

There were a number of able and useful men during this period. We will note a few examples from among the most prominent to give an idea of how the churches increased and to show the type of men that were in the Baptist ranks.

Hezekiah Smith — Hezekiah Smith was saved and joined a Baptist church as a young man. He was one of the first students in the first Baptist school in America, Hopewell Academy. After finishing there he went to Princeton where he graduated in 1762. In 1765 he received his M. A. Upon completion of his undergraduate work he made a fifteen month evangelistic tour of the south. He traveled over four thousand miles and preached one hundred and seventy-three sermons. He made another trip to the north where he organized a Baptist church at Haverhill, Massachusetts. He continued as pastor there for the rest of his life except for the time he was a chaplain in the American army during the Revolutionary War. During his ministry at Haverhill he made many trips on horseback throughout Maine and New Hampshire. He was responsible for the forming of thirteen churches in that area.

During one of his missionary trips into Maine he stopped at a public house to find lodging for the night. He was told of a dance that was to take place in the house that night. He planned to go to his room early but was met by a group going to the dance who urged him so he went with them planning to use the occasion for God's glory.

The people showed him great respect. Before commencing he thanked them for their kind treatment and stated that he had made it a principle of his life to always first ask the Lord's blessing upon everything that he undertook. He immediately began to pray. At the close of the prayer many were in tears. Hezekiah Smith began to speak and continued for some time. There was no dance that night. The final results were the conversion of several souls. A year later on another missionary tour to this region he met several who were converted the year before and was happy to find them living a Christian life. He was active in promoting Rhode Island College and helped start the Massachusetts Baptist Missionary Society and the Warren Association. He went to be with the Lord in 1805.

James Manning — James Manning was another leader among the Baptists. He went to Hopewell Academy where he was saved. He is said to be the first student of this first Baptist School in America. It was established by the Philadelphia Association under the headship of Isaac Eaton in 1756. It only continued eleven years but during that time did great good in training a number of useful men for the Baptists. James Manning went on to Princeton after finishing at Hopewell. He graduated from Princeton in 1762 as either first or second in his class. The Philadelphia Association desired to start a college in Rhode Island and needed a president. James Manning was selected and became the first president. The school began in 1766 with one student. At first it was called Rhode Island College but later Brown University after a generous contributor. He continued as president until his death in 1791. His labors were very important in the establishment of this school. He was also pastor of the First Baptist Church of Providence, Rhode Island, for many years.

Morgan Edwards — Morgan Edwards came to this country from England at the request of the Philadelphia church. He was a Welshman who had been trained at Bristol Seminary. He had several pastorates in the British Isles before coming to America. He was very important in the founding of Rhode Island College, having proposed the idea at a meeting of the Philadelphia Association. He also traveled much to promote the school among the churches and to raise money for it. As he traveled he collected materials for a Baptist history. Some of this material has been published and is very valuable.

Unitarianism in New England — In New England in the latter part of the eighteenth century many churches of other denominations were affected by Unitarianism. Baptist churches as a whole were not affected with this heresy.

Daniel Marshall — In the south the churches were greatly increased by men influenced directly or indirectly by the Great Awakening. The Philadelphia Association also had several churches in the south and several of their preachers had gone on preaching tours to strengthen the work. Daniel Marshall was a deacon of a Congregational church in Connecticut for some years. When he was thirty-eight he heard Whitefield preach and God used his message to change his life. He became very zealous and got rid of all earthly possessions and went to the Mohawk Indians as a missionary. Several Indians were converted but just as his labors were beginning to bear fruit an Indian war began forcing him to leave them. He moved to Winchester, Virginia, where he became acquainted with a Baptist church of the Philadelphia Association. Upon examining the Scriptures he became convinced of the Baptist beliefs and joined this church. He now became a Baptist preacher and with great zeal preached in Virginia, North Carolina, South Carolina, and Georgia. Several churches were established by him and many made professions of faith under his preaching.

Shubael Sterns — Shubael Sterns, the brother-in-law of Daniel Marshall, was converted under the preaching of George Whitefield. He became a Congregational minister but upon examining the Scriptures became convinced of Baptist doctrines and joined them. He had until this time lived in New England but after about three years he desired to preach the gospel in the south. He came to Virginia and North Carolina where the Lord blessed his ministry with the conversion of many souls.

Regular Baptists and Separate Baptists Unite — Shubael Sterns with Daniel Marshall went together to North Carolina where they organized the Sandy Creek Baptist Church. Sterns became the pastor and in seventeen years this church was the means of starting forty-two churches which sent out one hundred and twenty-five preachers.

These churches were called Separate Baptists. In Virginia there were only six Separate Baptist Churches in 1770 but by 1774 there were fifty-four. The Regular Baptists and Separate Baptists were united in 1787 on the basis of the Philadelphia Confession of faith.

Samuel Harriss — Samuel Harriss was born in Virginia in 1724 and rose to prominence. He was a colonel of the militia, a member of the legislature, captain of Mayo Fort, and judge of the court. He was saved and became a Baptist being baptized by Daniel Marshall. When he was saved he was in the process of building a large mansion in a style suitable for a man of his position. He turned this into a Baptist meeting-house and continued to live in his old home. He was very careful with his income and sought to use all of his surplus money for the Lord's work. He traveled throughout his state preaching the truth everywhere and suffering much for the truth. He is called "The Apostle of Virginia."

John Waller — During this period the Baptists suffered much persecution in Virginia. John Waller, a wicked man, who was known as "Swearing Jack Waller" because of his great use of profanity, was a persecutor of the Baptists. In time he was converted and became a Baptist preacher who suffered much for his convictions. The testimony of a Baptist preacher by the name of Louis Craig marks the beginning of the change in his life. Craig was brought before the grand jury, of which Waller was a member, for preaching. Craig said to the jury, "I thank you gentlemen of the grand jury, for the honor you have done me. While I was wicked and injurious you took no notice of me, but since I have altered my course of life and endeavor to reform my neighbors, you concern yourselves much about me." Waller was greatly impressed and began to attend the Baptist meeting and was saved.

After his conversion he, Craig, and James Childs were brought to court for preaching. The prosecuting attorney accused them before the court thus. "May it please your courtships, these men are great disturbers of the peace, they cannot meet a man upon the road, but they must ram a passage of Scripture down his throat." They were promised release if they stopped preaching which they refused to do. They sang a hymn as they were taken through the streets of Fredricksburg to prison.

Many Baptist preachers were imprisoned but this did not stop them. There are several accounts of them preaching through the bars to the crowds that assembled.

James Ireland — Cook says of James Ireland, A Baptist preacher,

> He had much to endure during his confinement. Several attempts were made to murder him. They first put powder under the floor of his room to blow him up, then tried to suffocate him by filling his cell with the fumes of burning brimstone, and finally with the aid of a physician poisoned him, but his life was spared. [R. B. Cook, *Op. Cit.*, p. 227.]

Persecution in Virginia — Virginia was perhaps the most intolerant of the colonies and this condition continued until the Revolution. Episcopalian clergymen were the only recognized ministers in the state. Anyone else who acted as a minister was severely punished. Baptists were forced to pay taxes to support the state church, the Episcopal.

Baptists and the American Revolution — The American Revolution was supported by the Baptists almost unanimously. A number of their preachers were chaplains. Their patriotism is illustrated by the following incident.

> Colonel Houghton was in the Hopewell Baptist Meeting-house, at worship, when he received the first information of Concord and Lexington, and of the retreat of the British to Boston with such heavy loss. His great grandson gives the following eloquent description of the way he treated the tidings: "Stilling the breathless messenger he sat quietly through the services, and when they were ended, he passed out, and mounting the great stone block in front of the meeting-house he beckoned to the people to stop. Men and women paused to hear, curious to know what so unusual a sequel to the service of the day could mean. At the first words a silence, stern as death, fell over all. The Sabbath quiet of the hour and of the place was deepened into a terrible solemnity. He told them all the story of the cowardly murder at Lexington by the royal troops; the heroic vengeance following hard upon it; the retreat of Percy; the gathering of the children of the Pilgrims round the beleaguered hills of Boston: then pausing, and looking over the silent throng, he said slowly: 'Men of New Jersey, the red coats are murdering our

brethren of New England! Who follows me to Boston?'
and every man of that audience stepped out into line, and
answered: 'I!' There was not a coward nor a traitor in old
Hopewell Baptist Meeting-house that day." [R. B. Cook,
Op. Cit., pp. 236-238.]

Cook tells of another Baptist patriot.

John Hart, of Hopewell, New Jersey, was a Baptist
and a signer of the Declaration of Independence. He was a
man of integrity and worth. He gave the grounds and built
upon it, the meeting-house for the Baptists of this town,
which still stands today. He represented New Jersey in the
First Continental Congress, in 1774. He risked and lost
everything — home and property, by putting his name to
that instrument. English troops hunted him, and he had to
flee for his life. One night he slept in a doghouse with the
dog. At another time he was forced to leave the bedside
of his dying wife. His native state has honored him and
has erected a granite monument to his memory, over his
grave at Hopewell, with this inscription upon it: "Honor
the Patriot's Grave." He was in 1776, elected speaker of
the New Jersey House of Assembly, to which position he
was elected for the third time. [R. B. Cook, *Op. Cit.*, pp.
236-238.]

Baptists Unjustly Taxed in Massachusetts — In
Massachusetts there was a state church, the Congregational,
and laws that forced Baptists and others to support it. The
days of the severe physical persecution were over there but
some unjust laws remained until 1833. An example of the
type of persecution in Massachusetts at this time is the
Ashfield case.

The town of Ashfield, Massachusetts was settled by
Baptists. In 1770, a few Congregationalists built a meeting
house, called a minister, and taxed the Baptists for his
support. The greater part of his salary of $1,000 came
from Baptists. Because they refused to pay this
burdensome tax, 398 acres of their land were seized,
together with their homes, cattle, crops, and graveyards —
constituting everything of many families, and sold to pay
the tax. Thus they were despoiled and made homeless, and
told to leave if they did not like it. The property was sold
far below its value, and the Orthodox minister was one of
the purchasers. [*Op. Cit.*, pp. 232-234.]

Baptists and Religious Liberty — This type of injustice continued after the Revolution and after the first amendment was added to the constitution. Because of such treatment the Warren Association sent Isaac Backus with a petition asking for Religious Freedom to the first Continental Congress in 1774. He was joined by delegates of the Philadelphia Association and several Quakers in presenting the petition. The delegates of the Congress promised to do what they could.

The Baptists in Virginia were more active than any group in disestablishing the state church and abolishing laws contrary to religious freedom in their state. They must also be given the honor of being most responsible for the first amendment to the constitution. Cathcart says,

> In 1789, a few months after Washington became President, "The Committee of the United Baptist Churches of Virginia" presented him an address written by John Leland, marked by felicity of expression and great admiration for Washington, in which they informed him that their religious rights were not protected by the new Constitution. The President replied that he would never have signed that instrument had he supposed that it endangered the religious liberty of any denomination, and if he could imagine even now that the government could be so administered as to render freedom of worship insecure for any religious society, he would immediately take steps to erect barriers against the horrors of spiritual tyranny. Large numbers were anxious about the new Constitution, and it had many open enemies. The Baptists who presented this address controlled the government of Virginia, and they were the warmest friends of liberty in America. They will suffer anything for their principles, and as they suspect the new Constitution, it must be amended to embrace their soul liberty, and secure their hearty support. A few weeks later James Madison, the special friend of Washington, who aided him five months before in composing his first inaugural address to Congress, rises in the House of Representatives and proposes the religious amendment demanded by the Baptists, with other emendations, and declares that "a great number of their constituents were dissatisfied with the Constitution, among whom were many respectable for their talents and their patriotism, and respectable for the jealousy which they feel for their liberties." This language applies to his Baptist constituents and their co-religionists over the land. He presses his scheme amidst violent opposition, and Congress

passes it. Two-thirds of the State Legislatures approve of
it, and it is a part of the Constitution.

Denominationally, no community asked for this
change in the Constitution but the Baptists. [William
Cathcart, *Op. Cit.*, pp. 107-109.]

The first amendment reads, "Congress shall make no
law respecting an establishment of religion, or prohibiting
the free exercise thereof, or abridging the freedom of speech
or of the press, or the rights of the people peaceably to
assemble and to petition the government for a redress of
grievances."

Before we leave this subject it would be well to note
this quotation dealing with the Baptist contribution in this
area. "We will now quote word for word some of the
statements of Troeltsch in which he refers to the great
importance of the Independent and Baptist movements."

Puritanism is not Calvinistic but Baptist. The
Calvinistic Puritan States of North America were indeed
democratic, but they not only knew nothing of freedom of
conscience but positively rejected it as godless scepticism.
There was freedom of conscience in Rhode Island alone;
but this State was Baptist, and was therefore odious to all
neighboring States as a seat of anarchy; its very great
organizer Roger Williams went right over to the Baptist
cause.

And likewise the second seat of freedom of
conscience in North America, the Quaker State of
Pennsylvania, was of Baptist origin. *The father of the
rights of man is thus not Protestantism properly speaking,
but the Baptist movement which it hated and expelled.*
The North American Baptist and Quaker movements
originated from the great religious movement of the
English revolution, that of the Independents. But this
Independent movement was itself most strongly permeated
with influence from the Baptist movement, which wrought
on England from Holland, the Continental refuge of the
Baptists, and from the American fugitives. In England the
Baptist movement in general experienced at least its most
important hour, when it abandoned its abstention from
politics and intervened to shape and bring forth a Christian
State. Cromwell's Commonwealth which planned to be a
Christian one realized this idea for a short time, and
however brief the period this magnificent creation lasted,
its effects on world history are extraordinary. For from
this mighty episode there have remained the great ideas of

the *separation of Church and State*, the toleration of *different* church communities alongside of one another, the voluntary principle in the formation of church bodies, and the freedom (at first, to be sure, relative) of conviction and opinion in all matters of philosophy and religion. In England there took root the old liberal theory that the inner personal life is beyond the reach of the State, a theory which then became ever more extended to more external things; here was reached the end of the mediaeval idea of civilization, and, in place of the compulsory culture based on the union of Church and State, there came into being modern, free individual culture. It was in the first place a purely religious idea, only soon secularized and overgrown with the rationalistic, sceptical, and utilitarian idea of toleration; but it alone, by its religious force, paved the way to modern liberty.

But this was not really the work of Protestantism, but of the newly quickened Baptist movement blended with radicalized Calvinism. The Baptist cause thus experienced a belated reparation for the boundless suffering which it, a religion of toleration and conscientious conviction, had to endure from all denominations in the sixteenth century. [Johannes Warnes, *Baptism*, pp. 290-291.]

Baptist Growth — By 1800 the Baptists numbered about 100,000 and had forty-eight associations. The first association in the south was the Charleston in South Carolina (1751) in New England the first was the Warren (1767). These new associations were patterned after the Philadelphia.

From 1800 to 1845 the Baptists grew greatly in numbers. They also began a foreign mission work and spread west as our country expanded. Some American Baptists had contributed to Carey's work in India and also to the spread of the Gospel among the Indians. However, the story of American Baptist foreign missions properly begins with Adoniram Judson and Luther Rice.

Adoniram Judson — Adoniram Judson was born the son of a Congregational minister. He attended Brown University and graduated at the head of his class in 1807. He became an infidel under the influence of a college friend but was shaken by his death so that he sincerely examined the Scriptures. He entered Andover Theological Seminary where he was saved and felt the Lord calling him to be a foreign missionary. Eventually he and others were sent out by the Congregationalists to India in 1812. On shipboard he studied the subject of baptism to be able to answer any inquiries on the subject that the English Baptists might make and to know how to deal with converts concerning this subject. His study finally led him to the conclusion that only believers are proper subjects and that the mode is immersion. After arriving he and his wife were baptized.

Luther Rice — Luther Rice was sent out on another ship by the Congregationalists for India. He studied the subject of baptism also and became convinced of Baptist views. After arriving he also became a Baptist. Judson and Rice were now in a foreign country without any support because of their convictions. They agreed between themselves that Judson would stay as a missionary and that Rice would return to tell the Baptists of their experience and to raise support for Judson.

The Beginning of the Triennial Convention — Rice returned to Boston where he told the Baptists his story. They agreed to support Judson and urged Rice to visit the Baptist churches throughout the country to interest them in foreign missions. A meeting of the Baptists was called which took place at Philadelphia in May of 1814. At this meeting "The General Convention of the Baptist Denomination in the United States for Foreign Missions" was formed. It was also called the "Triennial Convention" since it met every three years. Its first missionary was Judson and its first field was Burma where Judson went when the British East India Company would not let him work in India. Seven years after leaving America he had his first convert. The Judsons suffered much in establishing this work. The Lord blessed this work with many converts in later years. Judson also translated the Bible into the Burmese language. The Triennial Convention sent out other missionaries and new fields were opened in Siam, Hong Kong, Assam, and Liberia. There were also other Baptist mission works carried on in Germany, France, Denmark, and Greece.

Baptist Women — Usually little is said about the faithful work of Baptist women because it is the place of the men to lead in the work as the Bible teaches. However Baptist women have worked faithfully in the churches through the centuries. Their good work has been unnoticed usually but it has been very important. Their influence as mothers in training their children, as wives in helping their husbands, as church members in attending, helping the needy, teaching the women and children, and doing other good works has been without measure. Ann Judson is one of the best examples of the Baptist women. We would like to notice a few incidents in her life that show her faithfulness to the Lord.

Ann Judson — Ann Judson left with her husband Adoniram for the mission field as a Congregationalist. She and Adoniram studied the Baptist position that they might be prepared to meet the English Baptists in India. Ann was a woman of strong convictions and had to be sure the Bible taught anything before she would accept it. She wrote,

" 'I frequently told him, if he became a Baptist I would not.' But later she had to confess, 'We are now confirmed Baptists, not because we wished to be, but because truth compelled us to be . . . ' " [W. Mathews, *Dauntless Women*, p. 6]

Ann was very useful in the mission work. She labored with the women and children and aided her husband in many ways. One of her greatest contributions was the part she played in saving the Burmese translation of the New Testament. During the war between the English and Burmese when none of their property seemed safe and her husband was put in prison she concealed the translation in a very unusual way.

"On her next visit to the prison she carried a pillow so hard and uncomfortable that even the avarice of a Burmese jailer would not covet it. Into it she had sewn Adoniram's manuscript translation of the New Testament which it was unsafe for her to keep in the house. It was the only copy, and if it were confiscated by the Burmans, the concentrated toil of years would be lost." [*Op. Cit.*, p. 20.]

This does not tell all the story of the saving of this precious manuscript but it tells a very important part of the story.

Mrs. Judson's service to the Lord involved much suffering. She not only suffered with sickness but also in seeing her husband and children suffer. She saw her firstborn, a son, die; she saw her husband imprisoned and in great sickness. At one time Ann Judson was so sick she couldn't take care of the wants of her little daughter.

"Little Maria suffered most grievously because of Ann's illness, and neither a nurse nor a drop of milk could be found in the village to make up for the loss of her usual nourishment. 'Her cries in the night were heartrending,' wrote Ann, 'when it was impossible to supply her wants.' Sometimes when the jailers were induced by presents to allow Adoniram to come out of the prison, 'he carried poor little wailing Maria from door to door, still with but a few inches of chain between his shackled feet, a beggar at the breasts of pitying mothers.' 'Had it not been for the consolation of religion,' Ann wrote afterwards, 'and an assured conviction that every additional trial was ordered by infinite love and mercy, I must have sunk under my accumulated sufferings.' " [*Op. Cit.*, pp. 24-25.]

Her faithful service to the Lord came to a close at the early age of thirty-seven when she left this life to go to be with her Savior.

Johann Oncken and the German Baptist — In Germany there were many Baptists in the reformation period and before but they seemed to die out for many years until the nineteenth century. The mission work here began when a German boy by the name of Johann Oncken was taken to Great Britian by a Scottish merchant. Here he was converted and became a Congregationalist. In 1823 he was sent to Germany as a missionary of the Continental Society. After studying the Scriptures he came to Baptist views. In the winter of 1830-31 Captain Tubbs, an American sea captain, was ice bound at Hamburg during which time he stayed with the Onckens. Captain Tubbs was a member of the Sansom Street Baptist Church in Philadelphia. He and Oncken studied the Bible together and Tubbs explained the beliefs of the Baptists to him. Oncken stated that he believed Baptist churches were after the New Testament pattern and desired to be baptized. Captain Tubbs told his pastor about this. Professor Sears, a teacher of one of our Baptist schools, was told of this and when he was in Germany in 1834 for special studies looked up Oncken and baptized him and six others. They were organized into a church and Oncken became the Pastor. From this small beginning the modern German Baptists grew.

Disagreement in Bible Society over translating Baptizo
— One problem connected with the mission field was concerning the translation of the word baptizo. Our missionaries in translating the New Testament into the various languages translated it into the equivalent of immerse. The American Bible Society which was composed of members from several denominations had permitted the missionaries of all denominations to translate the word according to what they felt was correct. When a translation of a Baptist was refused for printing in 1835 because he followed this principle, the Baptists formed the American and Foreign Bible Society. Difference in this group caused a withdrawal of some to form the American Bible Union. Finally both agreed to disband and turn their work over to the American Baptist Publication Society and the American Baptist Missionary Union.

Baptists Expand at Home — After the Revolution the Baptists began to grow in Kentucky, Tennessee, Ohio, Illinois, and the rest of the middle west. A few churches were formed in this area just before the Revolution. Baptists from Virginia and North Carolina were among the first settlers in this region. Most of the work of establishing churches and winning people to the Lord in this area was carried on by men unknown by name today who felt called of God to go to the new region of the middle west. Vedder says,

> Many men of God went forth into this wilderness not knowing where they should find a night's lodging or their next meal, willing to suffer untold privations if they might only point some to the Lamb of God. It is impossible to estimate too highly or to praise too warmly the services of these men of strong faith and good works. Their hardships were such as we of the present day can hardly imagine. They traveled from little settlement to settlement on horseback, with no road save an Indian trail or blazed trees, fording streams over which no bridges had been built, exposed to storms, frequently sleeping where night found them, often prostrated by fevers or wasted by malaria, but indomitable still. [H. C. Vedder, *Op. Cit.*, pp. 321-322.]

John Mason Peck — One of the men that went into this area was John Mason Peck. He was ordained to the ministry in New York State in 1812 and soon became interested in home missions. The factor that God used to direct him to missionary work was Luther Rice's account of Judson's work on the mission field. In 1817 the Triennial Convention commissioned him to the area west of the Mississippi. He spent the rest of his life in the Mississippi valley establishing churches. He started a seminary and a college and set up a system of itinerant missions. The Triennial Convention was persuaded to stop his support about 1820 by the anti-mission Baptists. Later the Massachusetts Baptist Missionary Society made him its missionary at five dollars a week. Jonathan Going was sent by the Massachusetts brethren to examine the field and give a report. During this trip he and Peck decided upon an idea for a home mission society which came into existence as the American Baptist Home Mission Society in April 1832.

Anti-Missionary Baptists — During the early part of the nineteenth century the anti-missionary Baptists began. They believed that Sunday schools, mission societies, Bible societies, etc. were man-made and unscriptural. They believed that salvation was entirely of the Lord therefore they were opposed to the use of means in the salvation of the lost. Baptists have always believed that salvation was entirely of the Lord but also that we have been commanded to preach the gospel without which no one can be saved. Baptists believe that mission societies, Sunday schools, etc. are in harmony with New Testament principles and are proper methods to use. Missionary Baptists believe in election and in missions and do not believe they are in conflict when properly understood. There were several anti-mission groups. Some of them called themselves "Primitive" or "Old School." Others were called "Two-Seed-in the Spirit Predestinarian Baptists." These groups are often referred to by others as "Hard Shell Baptists."

Freewill Baptists — At the opposite extreme in theology we find a group of Baptists holding to Arminian views. There have been some churches holding to these sentiments in our country from colonial days. They have organized themselves into several groups that hold to some form of Arminian doctrine. They have been popularly called "Freewill Baptists." Their total number today is quite small compared to the "Missionary Baptists."

Alexander Campbell Troubles the Baptists — It was during this period that Alexander Campbell was to come on the scene and trouble the Baptists. Campbell, a Scotch Presbyterian, came to this country in the early years of the nineteenth century. He and his father and others formed a church at Bush Run in 1811. In time he became convinced of believer's baptism and he and most of the Bush Run Church were immersed by a Baptist preacher. The other members withdrew. In 1813 the Bush Run Church sought membership in the Redstone Baptist Association of Pennsylvania. After much debate and objections the church was admitted. At this time the main difference seemed to be that the ordinances were more than symbolic. Some didn't recognize his teachings at first for what they were. In time more differences were seen between him and the Baptists. He believed baptism was necessary to salvation. The salvation he preached was a salvation by one's own efforts. In time he attacked about all the practices of the Baptists, mission societies, ministerial calls, salaried preachers, associations, etc. Many followed him in Ohio, Kentucky, Tennessee and throughout the middle west. He and his followers were sometimes called "the Reformers." Later they were known as "Disciples of Christ," and "The Christian Church." Some called them "Campbellites" after their founder. Many preachers, churches, and associations condemned him and his unscriptural views. Churches and individuals who followed him were withdrawn from by the Baptists. His false doctrine did great harm to the churches of the middle west.

Early Baptist Schools — The Baptists began several schools in this period. Hopewell Academy (1756) was the first; Rhode Island College, later Brown University, (chartered 1764) was the second school. Newton Theological Institution, Waterville College (Colby College), Hamilton Literary and Theological Institution, Columbian College (George Washington University), and several others followed.

The Gospel Comes to the Negro Slave — Negroes were brought to the American continent as early as the seventeenth century but not in large numbers until early in the eighteenth century. Some people did not believe in preaching to them since they did not think they had a soul or because they thought that it would be dangerous to the institution of slavery. However some believed in preaching to them. The Baptists were among the most active in bringing the gospel to the Negro slaves. After the Great Awakening the Baptists grew in great numbers and many Baptists preached to the slaves on the plantations when allowed to do so. At first upon conversion they became members of white churches.

The First Negro Baptist Church in America — At the close of the eighteenth century another revival in America saw the conversion of many Negroes and the establishment of the first Negro Baptist church. This church was formed at Silver Bluff, South Carolina, between 1773-1775. Brother Palmer, an itinerant Negro Baptist preacher, came at times to this area and received permission to preach to the slaves on the John Galphin plantation. Several were saved and baptized by Brother Palmer and organized into a Baptist church. David George, one of the converted slaves, was trained by Brother Palmer and was chosen as the first pastor of the church.

George Lisle — George Lisle, a Negro Baptist preacher, came at times to preach to the Silver Bluff church. He was the slave of a Baptist deacon, Henry Sharpe, who was very kind to him. Sharpe took Lisle with him to church regularly which resulted in his salvation and baptism into a church in Burke county, Georgia. It was noted that Lisle had the gifts necessary for a minister and he was ordained. Henry Sharpe permitted him freedom to travel along the Savannah River to preach to the slaves on the plantations. The Lord blessed his ministry and Sharpe was so impressed that he gave Lisle his freedom so that he could preach without being hampered. After Sharpe's death his heirs tried to re-enslave Lisle but a British officer saved him from this ordeal. Lisle established a Negro Baptist church about 1779 in Savannah, Georgia and became the first pastor. When the British left Savannah at the end of the Revolutionary War Lisle went to Jamaica lest he be re-enslaved. Here he began to preach and several were saved. He organized these converts into a Baptist church which was the first Baptist church in Jamaica. Freedom was permitted for only the Anglican church so Lisle and several others were arrested and one was hanged. They were charged with "preaching sedition."

This action so stirred the Jamaican Assembly that they granted religious freedom and let Lisle and his brethren free. The Baptists grew so that by 1842 they sent forty missionaries to Africa.

Andrew Bryan — Andrew Bryan was baptized by George Lisle before he left America. He became the leader of the Savannah church and began to preach to white and Negro churches. The Savannah church was able to construct a building about this time. However the preaching and the activity of the church alarmed some of the slave owners and the church was forced to hold secret meetings in the swamps to avoid punishment. On one occasion Bryan and others were severely punished. Bryan was whipped and put in prison. In time he was released. The church continued to hold meetings and the persecution began to let up when one white eavesdropper heard the church praying for their persecutors and reported what he heard.

More Churches Established — New churches began to be established in both the north and the south. The Joy Street Baptist Church was started in 1804 in Boston; the Abyssinian Baptist Church was formed in 1808 in New York; the African Baptist Church was founded in 1809 in Philadelphia.

Lott Carey — One of the early, great, Negro Baptists was Lott Carey. Carey was born a slave in Virginia in 1780. He worked in Richmond at a tobacco warehouse and lived in vice. He was saved through the preaching of a white preacher and joined a white church, the First Baptist Church of Richmond, Virginia. In time he joined a Negro Baptist church and became an assistant pastor. He had a great interest in missions and started the Richmond African Missionary Society to raise offerings for missions in Africa. Lott Carey was sent out with Collins Teague as the first missionaries to Liberia in 1821. They were backed by Negro and white missionary societies in Richmond and by the Triennial Convention. Before they left, Carey, Teague, their wives, Teague's son and another couple going to settle in the country, were organized into the First Baptist church of Monrovia, Liberia, with Carey as pastor. These missionaries suffered great hardships for the Lord. Mrs. Carey died of tropical fever, Teague went on a trip and was never heard of again, Carey had to work often to supplement his income, and he was frequently sick. Carey died in 1828 after successfully beginning the Negro Baptist missionary work in Africa.

Nat Turner's Rebellion — In 1831 a sad event happened which hurt the Negro and his religious life. Nat Turner, a slave of unbalanced mind, believed he was sent of God to abolish slavery. He was able to convince some ignorant slaves of his mission and they began an uprising. He killed his master and his family and other slaves murdered a number of white people. This rebellion was put down and Turner was hanged. Since Turner was referred to as a Negro preacher all Negro preachers and assemblies were looked upon with fear by some. All of the southern states passed laws restricting the religious life of all Negroes. Some states passed more restrictive laws than others.

Negro Christians Restricted by Law — Religious assemblies were forbidden in many cases. In some cases they might have a meeting if certain conditions were met such as having a white minister in charge or having several white men there to observe. The Mississippi law of 1857 reads, "Free Negroes or Mulattoes, for exercising the functions of a minister of the gospel, on conviction may be punished by any number of lashes, not exceeding 39, on the bare back, and shall pay cost." Religious freedom was not allowed the Negro Baptist during the period from 1831 to the Civil War.

Laws Not Enforced in Every Case — Many southern people were opposed to these laws and protested but others had the Negroes carefully watched and enforced the law. Meetings were held even though it was very difficult. Some masters allowed their slaves to attend the white churches where they sat in a special part of the church such as the back or the galleries. Some allowed their slaves to have meetings. It was a very difficult time for Negro Baptists and other Negro Christians. During these times many Negroes fled to the north and the west.

The First Negro Baptist Associations — New Negro Baptist churches were started in northern cities and the old ones grew. The first Negro association was formed of some Ohio Baptist churches in 1836. This was the Providence Baptist Association. In 1838 another association was begun in Illinois, the Wood River Baptist Association. These two associations with other churches started the Western Colored

Baptist Convention in 1853. The American Baptist Missionary Convention was started in 1840 composed of Negro churches from New England and the middle Atlantic states. Many other associations were formed during the remainder of the century for fellowship, aid, and missionary work.

American Baptist Hymns — Baptists of America have contributed many hymns. Some of the best known are "Safe in the Arms of Jesus" by W. H. Doane, "He leadeth me: Oh, blessed thought" by J. H. Gilmore, "Shall we gather at the River" by Robert Lowry, "Sound the Battle-Cry" by W. F. Sherwin, and "My country, 'tis of thee" by Samuel F. Smith.

The Number of Baptists in 1845 — The period ends with the Baptists having about 9,000 churches and 700,000 members. The growth was very great during this 105 years when we remember that we began the period with about sixty churches and 5,000 members.

1845-1960: FROM THE DIVISION AMONG BAPTISTS OVER SLAVERY TO THE PRESENT

Introduction — This last period in American Baptist history will show how Baptists expanded from about 700,000 to 20,000,000, spread from the Mississippi River area to the Pacific Ocean, increased in educational institutions and foreign missions, and became divided into several large groups. The largeness of the movement forces us to examine the societies and conventions rather than individual churches and associations.

The Slavery Controversy Among Baptists — For some years prior to 1845 there had been a growing controversy over slavery. There were Baptists who owned slaves and believed it alright while other Baptists were greatly opposed to the practice.

The Triennial Convention had gone on record that the convention should stay out of the controversy and restrict themselves only to the work of missions. It had been further agreed that individuals in the convention could hold and advocate the position they believed right but that the convention should be neutral. Even though this controversy had arisen in the convention at times it was always possible to take care of it in such a way that the convention remained neutral and the members unified. In 1844 the Alabama State Convention asked the executive board of the General Convention if they would send a man to the foreign field as a missionary if he owned slaves. They replied that they wouldn't. A test case had been presented shortly before this to the American Baptist Home Mission Society by the Georgia Baptist Convention. The Home Mission Society had refused to send out the man in the test case because he owned slaves. In April of 1845 the Home Mission Society stated that they thought it best to have two separate organizations from then on, one to work in the North and the other in the South.

BAPTISTS OF THE SOUTH

Southern Baptist Convention Formed — On May 8, 1845 three hundred and ten delegates from Baptist churches of the south met at Augusta, Georgia, and began the Southern Baptist Convention. They formed two boards, the home mission board, and the foreign mission board. Later additional boards and agencies were to be established within the convention. The convention is composed of messengers from regular Baptist churches who have contributed to the work of the convention within the last year. These messengers which meet once a year are the ultimate authority in directing the various work of the convention.

Work of the Home Mission Board — The Home Mission Board of the Southern Baptist Convention sent out about nine hundred missionaries between 1845 and 1860. There were thirteen thousand converts and one hundred and seventy-nine new churches established. They worked among the settlers throughout the south and also among Negroes and Indians. A Chinese mission was maintained in San Francisco. The Civil War brought the home mission board practically to a stand still. After the war several of the Baptist agencies of the north helped the south to carry on their missionary work and there was discussion about the uniting of the Baptists of the north and the Baptists of the south. The conclusion was finally reached that the two groups should remain separate. The reconstruction period was a very difficult time in the south and funds were very low.

Dr. Tichenor — Dr. Tichenor became the

corresponding secretary in 1882. Under him the work prospered greatly. After five years of his leadership the missionaries had increased from 41 to 251. When he left office in 1899 there were about 750 missionaries. Torbet says,

> His remarkable leadership had virtually saved the Southern Baptist Convention; he had developed a definite plan of cooperative support of home mission work through regular giving; had established a church building department in 1884; . . . had fostered and built a Sunday school work until it was ready to go ahead on its own power under the present Sunday School Board organized in 1891. [R. G. Torbet, *Op. Cit.*, p. 391.]

The two World Wars and the depression had an effect on home missions. The home missionaries dropped considerably from a high in 1921 of 1,656 to 654. By 1945, 1,042 Southern Baptists had served as chaplains in World War II. By 1960 the Southern Baptist Convention had over 31,000 churches and better than 9,000,000 members. They also were working throughout the United States rather than just in the south.

Work of the Foreign Mission Board — The Foreign Mission Board of the Southern Convention began under the presidency of J. B. Jeter. The first mission field of this board was South China. Works were later started in Central China and North China. By 1900 the Southern board had about ninety missionaries in China, West Africa, Italy, Brazil, Mexico, and Japan. By 1948 there were 625 missionaries in nineteen countries. There were 1,381 missionaries in forty-four countries in every corner of the globe by 1959. These missions carry on the work of evangelism, establishing churches, running schools, publishing literature, and providing medical attention.

Southern Baptist Schools — The first school to train ministers for the Southern Convention was Southern Baptist Theological Seminary. It was started in 1859 and is now located in Louisville, Kentucky. Many able men among the Baptists have taught there such as J. P. Boyce, John A. Broadus, E. Y. Mullins, and A. T. Robertson. All have contributed books that have been very helpful to ministers.

John A. Broadus — The following story is told of one

of the first teachers at Southern Baptist Seminary. "Because
of the War the work of the Seminary was suspended from
June, 1862 to the fall of 1865. When the time came to
reopen the Seminary some thought that the end of the
Seminary seemed at hand. Dr. Broadus said, "Suppose we
quietly agree that the Seminary may die, but we'll die
first." The school did not die. When it opened, November
1, 1865, it had only seven students. In homiletics, Dr.
Broadus had only one student and he was blind. Dr.
Broadus gave that one student his best, and the careful
preparation of full lectures for that blind student laid the
foundation for the volume "Preparation and Delivery of
Sermons," which has wide use over the world as a text
book in Homiletics." [*E. C. Routh, Baptists on the March*,
pp. 72-73.]

    B. H. Carroll — Southwestern Baptist Theological
Seminary was begun in 1908 under the leadership of B. H.
Carroll. It is located in Seminary Hill, Texas. Carroll was
not only a great leader, teacher, and preacher among
Baptists in his day but also is a great influence in our day
through his many published sermons. His seventeen volume
Interpretation of the English Bible carries the student from
Genesis through Revelation giving a conservative, scholarly,
and practical explanation of the Bible. New Orleans Baptist
Theological Seminary was established in 1917. In recent
years several other seminaries have been started. Southern
Baptists have a number of academies, junior colleges,
colleges and universities. Some of their better known
universities today are Baylor, Furman, Wake Forest, Stetson,
and Hardin-Simmons.

    The Sunday School Board — The Publication Society
was started in 1854 and was connected with the convention
in 1863. In 1891 the Sunday School Board was begun to
take the place of the Sunday School Union. Both
Organizations have contributed much to Southern Baptist
growth.

    J. R. Graves — James Robinson Graves greatly
influenced the Baptists of the south during this period. He
was born in Chester, Vermont, in 1820. At fifteen he was
saved and joined a Baptist church. When he was twenty-one
he moved to Kentucky where he became the head of Clear
Creek Academy for four years. In 1845 he moved to

Nashville, Tennessee. Here he became the pastor of a Baptist church, started an Academy, and became the editor of the "Tennessee Baptist." To begin with, the circulation was small; but, by the start of the Civil War, it was the largest Baptist paper in the world and exerted a great influence upon Southern Baptists. He wrote a number of books and published many more. He was the founder of a publishing house and a Sunday school union. He was a very gifted preacher that had many professions of faith under his ministry. He was particularly strong in teaching Baptist distinctives concerning the church and its ordinances. After the Civil War his paper was moved to Memphis and called "The Baptist." During this century he is considered by many to have influenced Southern Baptists more than any other man. He died in Memphis in 1893.

The "Landmark" Movement — The "Landmark" movement was led by J. R. Graves. Graves emphasized the primacy of the local church and that the Baptists were the only true New Testament churches. These truths and the practices involved were emphasized from the time he became editor of the Tennessee Baptist in 1846. He believed that some were neglecting or violating these basic principles and so sought to emphasize them. The convention which had started in 1845 was also believed to encroach upon the primacy of the local church in the way it sent out missionaries. These principles were referred to as the old landmarks. Graves gave the movement its name when he entitled a tract of J. M. Pendleton "An Old Landmark Reset" in 1854. The emphasis and some applications were new to meet the situation of the time but the truths were old, as Baptist history reveals.

The American Baptist Association — After Graves' death some of the churches in this movement withdrew from the convention and several state Landmark associations were formed. The one in Arkansas began in 1902 under the leadership of Ben M. Bogard and W. A. Clark. Ben Bogard took the lead in calling for a meeting in 1905 to form a national association. This organization was called "The Baptist General Association." In 1924 the name was changed to the "American Baptist Association" when "The Baptist General Association," "The Baptist Missionary Association of Texas" and "The Oklahoma Baptist General

Convention" merged. The doctrines of the landmark Baptists and other missionary Baptists are essentially the same. The methods of cooperating with other churches in mission work seems to be the main difference. These churches have sent out missionaries and established a number of schools.

Baptist Missionary Association — In 1950 this Association (formerly the North American Baptist Association) began in Little Rock, Arkansas. These churches came out of the American Baptist Association over differences concerning administrative matters. This association has also grown very rapidly. They have missionaries on several fields and have several schools.

The World Baptist Fellowship — Another group of Baptist churches began in the twentieth century which originally were in the Southern Baptist Convention. Dr. J. Frank Norris was pastor of the First Baptist Church of Fort Worth, Texas, from 1910-1952 when he died. During this time he criticized the Texas Baptist General Convention and the Southern Baptist Convention because he believed there was liberalism in their schools and that the mission program was not Biblical. Some churches agreed with him and in 1934 they organized the Pre-millennial Baptist Missionary Fellowship. In 1935 Dr. Norris became pastor of Temple Baptist Church in Detroit in addition to his other church. His influence was felt in the north where some churches joined the fellowship. The name of the fellowship was changed in 1938 to the World Fundamental Baptist Missionary Fellowship. Missionaries were sent out and supported in several areas of the world. The Fundamental Baptist Bible Institute was started in Fort Worth to train students for Christian work in 1939. In 1945 the name was changed to the Bible Baptist Seminary. The name of the fellowship was changed again in 1950 to the World Baptist Fellowship. The "Fundamentalist" is the paper of the group. Until his death Dr. Norris was the leader of the movement.

The Baptist Bible Fellowship — In 1950 a group of men withdrew from the fellowship begun by Dr. Norris. The methods of Dr. Norris seem to be the main reason for the withdrawal. These men formed the Baptist Bible Fellowship in 1950, selecting Springfield, Missouri, as their center. Baptist Bible College was founded in Springfield the same year. A good number of students have graduated since then. Missionaries were sent out to many fields all over the world.

By 1958 they had 127 missionaries. A paper was started, the "Baptist Bible Tribune." Some of the churches in this fellowship are among the largest in the world. The first president of the fellowship was Dr. W. E. Dowell. The first president of their college and the pastor of Temple Baptist Church in Detroit is Dr. G. B. Vick. Temple Baptist Church is one of the largest Baptist Churches in the world. The World Baptist Fellowship and the Baptist Bible Fellowship are the same in doctrine. They hold to the same doctrines basically that other orthodox Baptists do. Their fellowships came about because of a belief that there was liberalism in the large conventions and that convention methods interfered with the autonomy of the local church.

Conclusion — During this period the Baptists of the south have had a remarkable growth making the south the largest center of Baptists in the world. Although the vast majority of Baptist churches in the south hold to the same basic doctrines Baptists have always held to, there have been some changes in doctrine in some schools and churches. The largeness of the convention and their methods have also been criticized in recent years as encroaching on the autonomy of the local church. Because of this some churches and pastors in the south have withdrawn from the Southern Baptist Convention while others have remained hoping to correct the situation.

BAPTISTS OF THE NORTH

The American Baptist Missionary Union — After the division over slavery the Triennial Convention changed its name to "The American Baptist Missionary Union." The Baptist churches of the north as a whole have sent out and supported their missionaries through this organization until about thirty years ago. Even though the Northern Baptists had to carry on this mission program by themselves the funds increased steadily or stayed about the same each year with few exceptions.

In 1846 there were 99 missionaries in Burma, Siam, China, Assam, India, Africa, France, Germany, Denmark, and Greece. By 1900 there were 474 missionaries.

During the latter half of the nineteenth century two policies were persued. The preaching of the gospel was emphasized to win converts rather than mission schools.

Education was not neglected though. The next policy was to develop self-supporting churches on the fields. These policies were very important in building a strong mission work. During this same period there was great growth on four fields. In Burma there were about 50,000 converts. In Assam there were 4,000 converts and in Africa 1,500 by 1900. In India among the Telugus the work was so discouraging that they considered closing the mission station. They continued on though and God blessed them with a great harvest of souls. A famine hit this part of India in 1876 and John E. Clough, a Baptist missionary who had some knowledge of engineering, sought to help the starving people. He contracted for the construction of several miles of a canal so that he could hire the needy natives. He made the native preachers overseers on the job and they read the Bible and preached to the natives when they weren't working. These natives carried the gospel to their homes. On December 25, 1877, 2,300 people professing faith in Christ asked to be baptized. By the close of the following year about 9,000 had been added to the church. On one day, July 3, 1878, 2,222 persons were baptized. By 1900 there were more than 200,000 native church members on all fields. There was a steady growth on the mission fields on into the early years of the twentieth century.

The Northern Baptist Convention Begins — In 1907 the Northern Baptist Convention was organized for the purpose of working out closer coordination for the Baptist societies of the north. The American Baptist Missionary Union and the other societies were all self-governing and had no organic connection with each other. They were to remain that way. The Northern Baptist Convention would enable the societies to cooperate in raising funds primarily.

The Missionary Union Changes its Name — The American Baptist Missionary Union changed its name to the American Baptist Foreign Mission Society in 1910. The Northern Baptist Convention recommended to the foreign society in 1912 that they not open any new fields for the present but that they do intensive work. The society followed this recommendation. Education was to be emphasized.

Foreign Missions in the 20th Century — During the twentieth century there has been growth on the mission

112

fields and opportunities for much greater growth but much
of the time the necessary funds were not available to send
out the needed missionaries. There has been strong criticism
of the foreign mission society during this century because of
what is termed the "inclusive policy." This policy allows for
the sending out of missionaries that are liberal as well as
conservative in doctrine.

*The Work of the American Baptist Home Mission
Society* — The American Baptist Home Mission Society
continued to send missionaries into the west. The
missionaries followed the railroads to begin missions which
were later organized into churches. The society also aided
new churches in building meeting houses. Hundreds of
churches and their buildings came into existence due to the
society. The Home Mission Society didn't work in the south
between 1846-1862 to avoid tension over the slavery
question with the Southern brethren. After 1862 they
resumed their work in the South. Later agreements were
worked out between the Home Mission Board of the
Southern Baptist Convention and the Society which made
better harmony among them in areas where they both
worked. The division of territory was made even clearer
with the beginning of the Northern Baptist Convention with
its sectional name. The American Baptist Home Mission
Society worked in harmony with the convention even
though independent for which reason the word "Northern"
stuck with them. Work was done among Indians, Negroes,
immigrants, and the people of Central America. During this
period a policy of interdenominational cooperation was
followed lest there be too many churches in one area. This
policy came with the beginning of the Federal Council of
Churches of Christ in America which the Northern Baptist
Convention joined in 1908 when it began. The name of this
organization has been changed to the National Council of
the Churches of Christ in the U. S. A.

The American Baptist Publication Society — The
American Baptist Publication Society began in 1824 as the
Baptist General Tract Society. It has played an important
role in Baptist growth by supplying Sunday school
literature, tracts, Bibles, and books.

Schools of the American Baptist Convention — The
Northern Baptist Convention, which was renamed the

American Baptist Convention in 1950, has sixty-five schools of all types that cooperate with it. Some of their better known universities and colleges are Bucknell, University of Chicago, Colgate, and Colby. Liberalism has taken over in many of their schools today. Because of this situation several schools were started in this century so that ministers could be trained according to the conservative beliefs of the Baptists of former days.

Influencial Writers — There were several writers and teachers that had a great influence on Baptists during this period. William Cathcart has written several works but perhaps the Baptist Encyclopedia is his greatest contribution. Alvah Hovey edited the American Commentary plus writing other works. The American Commentary is written by a number of different authors, all of whom are Baptists. A. H. Strong has given us his work on theology which is widely used today.

The Baptist World Alliance — The Baptist World Alliance began in 1905 as an organization to promote fellowship and cooperation among Baptists around the world. Most of the large Baptist groups are members. It meets once every few years.

Liberalism Invades Some Schools — During the twentieth century there have been strong differences among the Baptist of the north resulting in the withdrawal of many churches from the American Baptist Convention.

Some of the schools connected with the convention were strongly affected by evolution and higher criticism around the turn of the century. As a result many denied the inspiration of the Bible, the Deity of Christ, the orthodox view of the atonement and conversion plus many other beliefs that Baptists have always held. Many times those believing these liberal and unorthodox views continued to use the terms of the Scripture and of orthodoxy but giving them their own meanings. The true nature of these liberals was often hidden to most Baptists because of this practice. Even though those holding these unscriptural views were a small minority they were able to wield great influence because they held many important positions in the schools and in the convention and other Baptist agencies.

New Conservative Schools Begin — Liberalism was met by new schools that were begun to train ministers in conservative Baptist theology. Northern Baptist Theological Seminary was started in 1913 in Chicago since the Divinity School of the University of Chicago was liberal and unacceptable to the majority of the Baptists of the area. Other schools were started also.

Leaders in the Fight Against Liberalism — A number of men recognizing what was happening protested and sought to correct the situation. Some of the leaders in this effort were W. B. Riley, John Roach Straton, J. C. Massee, and Curtis Lee Laws. In 1920 the Fundamental Fellowship of the Northern Baptist Convention was begun. This was the start of a battle which has existed to the present day.

The "Inclusive Policy" — The fundamentalists sought to get the convention to accept a confession of faith from time to time but without success. Investigations were called for but they were unable to accomplish much. The "inclusive policy" of the foreign mission society was attacked but to no avail. As long as the convention was "inclusive" having liberals and conservatives, then a society supported by it should be also, some thought. The foreign mission society denied that it followed an "inclusive policy" as stated by its critics. They stated that they followed an "evangelical policy" that was based on the "Anderson Statement" of 1924. The "Anderson Statement" gave the policy that would be followed in sending out missionaries. Certain doctrinal qualifications were made in this statement. The Fundamentalists did not believe this statement was clear enough to keep liberals from being sent out. They also believed that there was definite evidence that liberals had been sent out and that the mission society was following an "inclusive policy."

The General Association of Regular Baptist Churches — There were many withdrawals of churches through the years because of the liberalism, the connection with the Federal Council of Churches, and the dangers to the independence of the churches. One of the major ones was in 1932 when about fifty churches withdrew and the General Association of Regular Baptist Churches was formed. This Association now numbers about 900 churches. One of the main leaders from the beginning has been Dr. Robert Ketcham. They accepted the New Hampshire Confession of Faith with a clear statement on the premillennial return of Christ.

It has no schools or missions but does recommend some that meet certain standards of doctrine and policy. The schools that they recommend are Baptist Bible Seminary of Johnson City, New York, which is the largest having over 400 students, Cedarville College, Grand Rapids Baptist Theological Seminary, Los Angeles Baptist Theological Seminary, Western Baptist Bible College and Theological Seminary, and Omaha Baptist Bible Institute. They approve of the following missions: Association of Baptists for World Evangelism, Evangelical Baptist Missions, Baptist Mid-Missions, Fellowship of Baptists for Home Missions, and Hiawatha-Land Independent Baptist Mission. "The Baptist Bulletin" is the official monthly magazine of the association.

The Conservatives were Optimistic — The conservative churches that remained continued to try to put the liberalism out of the convention. There was optimism among Conservatives that they were gaining.

> In 1941 fundamentalists were still optimistic and believed that they had made more progress than subsequent events proved. The Baptist Bulletin (9-1943) speaking editorially, said, "In 1941 Dr. Bradbury wrote a letter to an eastern pastor in which he says, 'Under the circumstances it would not be wise for us openly to boast for there is no sense in stirring up the enemy, but to give you some idea of what has been accomplished, we have gained control of the Foreign Mission Board; have an approximate control of the Home Mission Boards; have reformed the Publication Society; have built up three of our largest seminaries and training schools in Eastern, Northern, and Gordon, besides establishing Western and strengthening Central; ... by our attacks have reduced Rochester, Crozer and Chicago University Schools to a mere nominal status; obtained fundamentalist representation on all Boards and Committees of the Convention and placed an increasing number of fundamentalists in State Secretary and other secretarial positions. As a corporate ministry the fundamentalist movement in the Northern Baptist Convention has brought about tremendous changes and has justified the purpose of those who stay within the ranks to fight the battle through to a finish." This viewpoint was shared by many fundamentalists of that period. [C. E. Tulga, *The Foreign Missions Controversy in the Northern Baptist Convention*, pp. 101-102.]

Dr. Earl V. Pierce, a leader of the Fundamental Fellowship and a man in a position to know, stated in December of 1943 that he believed 75% of the preachers in the Northern Baptist Convention and 85% of the laity were conservatives. But the liberals were still able to control the convention.

Methods Used to Counteract Liberalism — The Fundamental Fellowship's name was changed to the Conservative Baptist Fellowship of Northern Baptists. This fellowship sought to inform Baptists of liberalism by putting out vast amounts of literature. The Case booklets of Dr. Chester E. Tulga and other literature went far and wide in this program of education. Many were made aware of the problem but not enough were convinced and willing to take the necessary action in the convention to correct it.

Many conservative Baptists in the past had designated their offerings to conservative missionaries of the American Baptist Foreign Mission Society but this didn't change anything. Enough money came in undesignated that all missionaries could still be supported. Some thought that a new mission society that was entirely conservative, if accepted as one of the societies of the convention, would receive all offerings from conservatives in time. Conservative money would not in any way help liberals if given to the new mission society which would mean a great blow to liberalism. The fundamentalists formed the Conservative Baptist Foreign Mission Society in December of 1943. However the new society was not recognized as being a Northern Baptist Convention society. The Conservative Baptist Foreign Mission Society operated separately and within five years sent out over 100 missionaries to thirteen countries.

The Conservative Baptist Association of America — In May of 1947 the Conservative Baptist Fellowship organized the Conservative Baptist Association of America and in 1948 the Conservative Baptist Home Mission Society. Churches of the Conservative Association must accept the doctrinal statement which follows the principles of the Baptists of past centuries. The churches must also agree not to support any society that follows the inclusive policy. The association has grown to over 1,000 churches in its short history and has a large and vigorous missionary program. The conservative Baptists also have several schools. They are Central Conservative Baptist Theological Seminary, Minneapolis, Minnesota; Western Conservative Baptist Theological Seminary, Portland, Oregon; Conservative Baptist Theological Seminary, Denver, Colorado; The San Francisco Conservative Baptist Theological Seminary, San Francisco, California; Baptist Bible College, Denver, Colorado; Judson Baptist College, Portland, Oregon; and Pillsbury Conservative Baptist Bible College, Owatonna, Minnesota.

Many Conservatives Stay in the American Baptist Convention — Many conservative churches and individuals remained in the convention, still believing something could be done to change the strong liberal influence. Others remained seemingly unaware of the liberal problem. There have also been many conservative churches that have withdrawn from the convention but have not become a part of either the G. A. R. B. or the Conservative Association. There have also been many new Baptist churches organized that have never been connected with the convention or any other large body of Baptists.

The Beginning of Negro Baptist Schools — After the Civil War the Negro Baptist churches began to develop and grow. Freedom from slavery and missionary work carried on by Baptists of the North and South helped to improve their situation considerably. Schools were started among them, supplying usually a very elementary education. In time more advanced schools and colleges were started. Henry Martin Tupper, a white Union soldier, is an example of the missionaries sent out to work among the Negroes. After the war the American Baptist Home Mission Society sent out Tupper. He came to Raleigh, North Carolina, where in time he organized a Baptist church and led in constructing a log cabin. He started a school using this church building. Later he and the students made a kiln and baked bricks to make the first school building. From this small beginning came Shaw University.

National Baptist Convention U. S. A., Inc. — There had been many organizations but none had really been effective in foreign missions. In 1880 the Foreign Mission Convention of the United States of America was begun. W. W. Colley, a Negro minister, had been sent out as a missionary to Africa by the Southern Baptist Convention. When he returned he led in the calling and organizing of the Foreign Mission convention. The convention began with 151 delegates from eleven states. Brother Colley became the first Corresponding Secretary. After three years he went to Africa as a missionary with five others. The National Baptist Convention was started in 1886 for other cooperative efforts of Negro Baptist churches. It was composed of delegates from all parts of the nation. The Baptist National Educational Convention was established in 1893. For more effective work these three combined in 1895 into the National Baptist Convention of the United States of America, Inc. This convention has several boards among which are the Foreign Mission Board, the Home Mission Board, the Educational Board, and the Publishing Board. This convention is composed of delegates from Negro Baptist churches having a total membership of about 5,000,000. This is the second largest Baptist body in the world.

The Lott Carey Missionary Convention – There have been two divisions in this convention. Neither came about because of doctrinal differences but because of policy. The first group withdrew and formed the Lott Carey Missionary Convention in 1897. This division began when the National Baptist Convention decided to publish their own literature when it didn't seem necessary or wise at that time to some. The division was completed when the headquarters of the Foreign Mission Board was moved.

The National Baptist Convention of America Unincorp. – The second division came about in 1915. The Publishing Board under the leadership of R. H. Boyd had become very successful in getting out materials and was also very prosperous. The Board was incorporated without any mention of its connection with the National Baptist Convention and its materials were copyrighted in Boyd's name. The convention, trying to correct the situation, learned that Boyd considered the convention as having no claim on the Publishing Board. Because of this difference of opinion Boyd took the Publishing Board out of the convention and made it a part of a new convention, The National Baptist Convention of America Unincorporated. Since the publishing board started from nothing and became very successful under his able leadership he thought it only right to have it set up as he set it up. There has been discussion in recent years about the possiblity of these two conventions uniting.

Negro Baptist Schools — The National Baptist Convention Inc. in cooperation with the Southern Baptist Convention operate the American Baptist Theological Seminary for the training of ministers. There are a number of schools of higher learning that are closely connected with the convention. The National Baptist Convention started another publishing board which supplies all types of literature for the churches.

Negro Baptist Foreign Mission Work — The missionary board of this convention has thirty-five full-time missionaries and over seven hundred part-time assistants. Its main field has been Africa where they have had over 400,000 conversions and have established more than 1,200 Baptist churches. In recent years they have sent missionaries to other fields. Mission work is now carried on in Liberia, Nigeria, Nyasaland, South Africa, Ghana, Sierra Leone, Southern Rhodesia, Bahama Islands, Nicaragua, Okinawa, Japan, and India. Negro Baptists have had a great influence upon their race for good.

Swedish-American Baptist Beginnings — The Swedish Baptists in the United States look to 1852 as their beginning. Gustaf Palmquist, a teacher and preacher, baptized three fellow immigrants in the Mississippi River in that year and started a Baptist church in Rock Island, Illinois. A number of Baptist churches made up mainly of Swedish immigrants were established in the next few decades. Most of these churches began in the middle west. Many of these people came because of persecution in their native land. An example of this is seen when in 1853 F. O. Nilsson and twenty-one other Baptists left Sweden and came to America because of persecution. The work was hard but many men and women worked faithfully and the Lord blessed with more converts and churches.

The Baptist General Conference of America — The first conference of Swedish Baptists was held in 1856 at the Rock Island, Illinois church. Its purpose was Bible study and spiritual growth and it was attended by delegates from several churches. Other conferences were organized in the next few years. The Baptist General Conference of America was begun in 1879 at Village Creek, Iowa. This conference was first called The Scandinavian Baptist General Conference. Later its name was changed to the present designation.

The Work of the General Conference — This conference has grown to over 500 churches and about 70,000 members. Today they carry on mission work in Alaska, Mexico, Argentina, Brazil, Ethiopia, India, Japan, Philippines, Burma, and the United States. They have a college and seminary which dates back to 1871, Bethel College and Theological Seminary. They also publish materials to aid in their Sunday school work. The official organ of the Baptist General Conference is The Standard.

German-American Baptist Beginnings — In the first half of the nineteenth century many German immigrants came to our country. There were various reasons for their coming but political freedom and religious freedom were prominent. Several German Baptist churches were formed independently and simultaneously in various parts of the country. The oldest church of this group was formed in 1843 in Philadelphia, Pennsylvania. Anton Fleischmann baptized five and they were organized into "The German Church of the Lord That Meets on Poplar Street." Fleischmann was saved in Switzerland. As he crossed Lake Geneva in a boat a Christian witnessed to him and gave him a tract. He became convinced of Baptist views and came to America to preach the gospel to his native countrymen at the suggestion of George Mueller. Some who came to this country had been saved and baptized in Germany under the influence of Oncken.

Christopher Shoemaker was a Pietist Dutch pastor in St. Louis who became convinced of the Scripturalness of Baptist baptism as he watched a group of Negroes baptize in the Mississippi River. He went home to study the subject in the Bible and became thoroughly convinced. John Mason Peck baptized him and he and sixteen others began a Dutch-German Baptist church in St. Louis.

The North American Baptist General Conference — These German Baptist churches scattered across America were called to a conference in 1851 at Philadelphia. They began a Publication Society which put out many useful materials. A German department was started at Rochester Theological Seminary under the leadership of August

Rauschenbusch to train German ministers. Later it became a separate school and was moved to Sioux Falls, South Dakota. A second conference was begun in 1859 to take care of the churches farther west. It began in Springfield, Illinois, and was known as the Western Conference, the older as the Eastern Conference. In 1865 a general conference was started in Wilmot, Ontario. This is known as the North American Baptist General Conference. A missionary society was begun later which has sent out many missionaries to the Cameroons, Japan, and to work among the Indians and Spanish Americans. The General Conference today is composed of about 300 churches totaling about 50,000 members. They join together to send out missionaries, put out literature, train ministers, and to do other benevolent works.

There are other Baptist groups that are primarily of one nationality but they are quite small compared to the Swedish and German groups.

Unaffiliated Baptists — There is a large group of Baptists in the United States that are not affiliated with any major body. Some of these churches have never been connected with any of the Baptist conventions or associations. It is surprizing how many Baptist churches are in this group. They are found in every part of the nation, not in just one or two areas. Some send out their own missionaries and support them with the aid of other such churches. Baptist Faith Missions of Detroit, Michigan and Latin-American Baptist Missions of the Central Baptist Church, Little Rock, Arkansas are examples of such missions. They have also started many small schools, usually on the Bible school level. Mountain State Schools of Alderson, and West Virginia, Lexington Baptist College of Lexington, Kentucky, are examples of these schools. The main reasons why they do not join the larger Baptist bodies for cooperation in missions, education, and other joint efforts are the following: (1) They already have their missionaries and other projects to support. (2) They believe that the larger groups sometimes infringe upon the independence of the churches. (3) They know that in some of these bodies there is liberalism and they cannot cooperate with such a mixture. This group is growing and is having a greater influence upon Baptists than most realize.

Conclusion

A SUMMARY

To summarize we have seen that the churches of the New Testament are what we would call Baptist churches today. This kind of church began in the personal ministry of the Lord Jesus Christ and has continued until the present. Our main reason for believing this is that the Lord promised that His church would continue. This promise is confirmed by historical evidence. We do not say that every church calling itself Baptist is a New Testament church. The name or affiliation is not the test of a New Testament church. The test is, does it follow the Bible. Not all churches called Baptist can pass this test. There have been some differences among Baptist churches from the beginning down to our time but these differences have not kept them from being New Testament churches. You can see this in the New Testament and in the middle ages among the Waldenses and today among us. There are doctrines and practices though that we must hold which we have stated in the introduction of this book.

During most of their history the Baptists have been greatly persecuted. Until religious toleration came in the seventeenth century we had few historical documents. Baptists were called by various names during their history but their doctrine remained essentially the same. Most of the information about them comes from their enemies. Since the coming of toleration Baptists have flourished mainly in the English speaking world. The English and American Baptists have been mainly responsible for the establishing of Baptist churches around the world in the last two centuries.

LESSONS FROM HISTORY

Since God often used the history of the Jewish nation

in the Old Testament to teach the Jews certain lessons, we believe that we can learn certain lessons that will be most beneficial by examining our history. There are examples to follow and also dangers to guard against. We urge each reader to note carefully the history in this light. There are however two grave dangers that we would particularly call to your attention that face us today.

Liberalism — One grave danger that faces us now is liberalism in theology. Some who call themselves Baptists deny the full inspiration of the Bible, the real Deity of Christ, the substitutionary sufferings of Christ for our sins, and many other doctrines. Such beliefs cannot bring about conversions or a new life in Christ. They cannot build New Testament churches but only tear them down. To associate ones self with such as believe these teachings to carry out the Lord's work is eventually fatal. The very objectives of the conservative Bible believer are destroyed by the liberal with which he works. Baptists must withdraw from all associations with liberals or face tremendous loss.

Evangelistic Methods — Another grave danger that faces us is a striving for conversions by methods that are not Biblical. Such methods usually produce superficial professions of faith. Many of our churches are filled with such conversions and they are sickly and weak spiritually even though they often think they are strong. This striving for numbers unscripturally is often motivated by a desire to be recognized by others as successful. Success is measured in numbers according to them. Great pressure is often put on crowds to make some decision, any decision. Tricks are sometimes used to get decisions. Many conservative ministers are guilty of using these unbiblical methods. Superficial conversions build superficial churches that produce superficial results. Such methods will ruin Baptists. We find mass evangelism in the Bible but it is brought about by the Holy Spirit using men who faithfully preach all of the truth of God. Baptists must be faithful in preaching and teaching the Scriptures and leave the results to God if they are to remain New Testament churches.

The Answer — These dangers and others not mentioned can be counteracted by following what the Lord commanded. He has urged us to believe and stand for the things He taught and to practice holy living. As individuals and churches we need to heed what the Lord says. Unless there is Bible study and Bible preaching we will not know what the Lord wants us to believe and practice. Fifteen minute sermons once a week that deal in generalities will not build up the churches. We need to return to an emphasis on preaching and teaching the Bible or we should take the pulpit from the center of the platform. We need to return to family and individual prayer and Bible reading. We need to proclaim all of the truth, the deep and the simple, the offensive and the compelling. The Lord Jesus Christ did. In love we need to stand for the truth and not compromise it and minimize it. Individuals and churches need to judge themselves. Christians ought to live like Christ wants them to and a church ought to act like a body of Christ. Church members that act like the world should be disciplined. Baptist churches are the strongest when they follow the Lord's commands on discipline. How can a Christian serve the Lord when he does not live like a Christian? He cannot. How can a Baptist church serve the Lord when there are divisions among them and members that deny by their lives what is professed and preached? She cannot. How can the world we are to witness to have any confidence in such individuals and such churches? It cannot. Baptists need a better testimony. We can have it by an emphasis on Bible preaching, church discipline, and holy living.

Confidence in the Future — We are confident that the Lord will bring us through these dangers and others as He has brought us through many dangers in the past. Baptists have had a glorious history and look forward to a glorious future, for the Lord has promised that "the gates of Hell shall not prevail against" His church.

A Census Table Of Baptists

AFRICA

Cameroon	48,185
Central African Republic	18,589
Liberia	22,500
Mozambique	30,000
Nigeria	106,280
Rwanda	13,811
South Africa	51,043
Zaire Republic	465,184
Other Countries	52,674
Total	808,266

ASIA

Bangladesh	21,000
Burma	253,128
China	123,000
(Mainland 1951 figure)	
China (Taiwan)	11,587
Hong Kong	25,208
India	703,275
Japan	32,320
Korea	13,678
Other Countries	20,283
Total	1,203,479

CENTRAL AMERICA

Bahamas	30,521
Cuba	16,235
Haiti	130,000
Jamaica	55,000
Other Countries	30,229
Total	261,985

EUROPE

England	173,708
Germany, D D R	24,019
Germany, West	74,235
Hungary	19,600
Netherlands	10,329
Romania	120,000
Scotland	16,250
Sweden	45,688
U. S. S. R.	550,000

(The government lists 550,000;
other figures go as high as 4,000.000)

Wales	72,097
Other Countries	55,680
Total	1,161,606

NORTH AMERICA

Canada	174,264
Mexico	43,849
United States	27,309,358
Total	27,527,471

SOUTH AMERICA

Argentina	22,237
Brazil	389,970
Chile	11,885
Other Countries	18,767
Total	442,859

SOUTHWEST PACIFIC

Australia	48,621
Indonesia	17,833
New Guinea	13,500
New Zealand	17,287
Philippines	51,324
Other Countries	899
Total	149,464
Grand Total	31,555,130

UNITED STATES
Largest Baptist Groups

American Baptist Association	786,536

American Baptist Convention	1,353,129
Baptist Bible Fellowship	1,000,000
Baptist General Conference of America	108,494
Conservative Baptist Association of America	300,000
General Association of Regular Baptist Churches	192,495
National Baptist Convention of America	3,500,000
National Baptist Convention, U. S. A., Inc.	6,300,000
North American Baptist Association	250,000
(Name changed in 1968 to Baptist Missionary Association of America)	
North American Baptist General Conference	54,997
Progressive National Baptist Convention, Inc.	550,000
(formed in 1961)	
Southern Baptist Convention	11,870,619
World Baptist Fellowship	220,000
U. S. Total	26,486,270

Notes on Table

1. Baptists are found in more than 130 countries.
2. The figures on the countries were gathered in January 1972 by the Baptist World Alliance. The figures on the largest Baptist groups were gathered from various sources from 1969 to 1972. Some are estimates.
3. Many Baptists did not report so this is not a complete tabulation.
4. The figures on the United States represent only the largest Missionary Baptist bodies.
5. There are some churches in the United States that are in more than one convention. Because of this and the many unaffiliated Baptists an accurate total of the Baptists in the United States is not possible.